REINCARNATION AND KARMA

REINCARNATION AND KARMA

Two Fundamental Truths of Human Existence

Five lectures given during January to March 1912
in Berlin and Stuttgart

RUDOLF STEINER

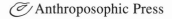 Anthroposophic Press

The original German texts of these lectures are published under the title: *Wieder-verkörperung und Karma und ihre Bedeutung für die Kultur der Gegenwart.* (Volume No. 135 in the Bibliographical Survey, 1961), by Rudolf Steiner Verlag, Dornach, Switzerland, 1961.

Translated from shorthand reports, unrevised by the lecturer,
by D.S. Osmond, C. Davy, and S. and E.F. Derry.

First published in English by Anthroposophical Publishing Company, London, 1960.

Introduction copyright © Herbert Hagens, 1992.

Published by Anthroposophic Press,
RR 4, Box 94 A1, Hudson, New York, 12534.

Library of Congress Cataloging-in-Publication Data

Steiner, Rudolf, 1861–1925.
    [Wiederverkörperung und Karma und ihre Bedeutung für die Kultur der Gegenwart. English]
    Reincarnation and karma : two fundamental truths of human existence / Rudolf Steiner; [translated from shorthand reports, unrevised by the lecturer, by D.S. Osmond, C. Davy, and S. and E.F. Derry].
        Translation of : Wiederverkörperung und Karma und ihre Bedeutung für die Kultur der Gegenwart.
        Five lectures given Jan.–Mar. 1912 in Berlin and Stuttgart, Germany, to members of the Theosophical Society.
        ISBN 0-88010-366-3
        1. Anthroposophy. 2. Reincarnation. 3. Karma I. Title.
BP595. S894W4713   1992   92-28594
299'.935—dc20   CIP

10 9 8 7 6 5 4 3 2

Printed in the United States of America

CONTENTS

Berlin, March 5, 1912

Reincarnation and karma: the fundamental
ideas of the anthroposophical world conception.
The strengthening of the moral life.

INTRODUCTION

by Herbert Hagens

On February 4, 1992 Vaclav Havel, then President of Czechoslovakia, addressed the World Economic Forum at Davos, Switzerland. He outlined the dangers facing our global civilization and called for solutions based on recognition of the spirit:

> The world, too, has something like a spirit or soul. That, however, is something more than a mere body of information that can be externally grasped and objectified and mechanically assembled. Yet this does not mean that we have no access to it. Figuratively speaking, the human spirit is made from the same material as the spirit of the world. Man is not just an observer, a spectator, an analyst or a manager of the world. Man is a part of the world and his spirit is part of the spirit of the world. We are merely a peculiar node of being, a living atom within it, or rather a cell that, if sufficiently open to itself and its own mystery, can also experience the mystery, the will, the pain, and the hope of the world.

Havel proclaimed that the hope of the world depends upon the mediation between the "mysterious power" within each human being and the "mysterious power of the world's being." People everywhere continue to respond most warmly to Havel's message of global conscience.

But the essential problem remains: how do we become "sufficiently open" to our own mystery and thereby to the wider mystery of the world? How do we learn to mediate internal and external, microcosmic and macrocosmic?

In response to questions like these, Rudolf Steiner (1861-1925) developed modern spiritual science, which he called Anthroposophy. He defined his Western esoteric teaching as "a path of knowledge to guide the spiritual in the human being to the spiritual in the universe." Anthroposophy is based on a profound understanding of the bodily, soul, and spiritual natures of the human being and it helps the seeker to develop a truly comprehensive self-knowledge, which includes coming face-to-face with the truth of reincarnation and karma. Awakening to one's spiritual core can happen only when the pupil learns to transform everyday thinking, feeling, and willing into active soul forces (capacities) through consistent meditative practice. This is the path to the kind of openness Havel is promoting.

Early in 1912, Rudolf Steiner gave the five lectures in *Reincarnation and Karma* to members of the Berlin and Stuttgart branches of the Theosophical Society. At the time he was still head of the German section of the Theosophical Society. During the previous summer in Munich, Steiner's Mystery Drama, *The Soul's Probation*, had been produced for the first time. This play was one of the earliest attempts to portray a community of spiritual seekers who were re-experiencing their previous incarnations. In connection with these productions, Steiner often spoke on the topic of past lives and related questions of destiny. In the five lectures printed here he gives specific meditative exercises that make it possible for pupils to experience the truth of reincarnation and karma for themselves.

Like Havel, Steiner identified the symptoms of our troubled times and offered a compelling solution:

The complexity of external life will steadily increase and however many activities are taken over from human beings in the future by machines, there can be very few lives of happiness in this present incarnation unless conditions quite different from those now prevailing are brought about. And these different conditions must be the result of the human soul being convinced of the truth of reincarnation and karma. (Lecture Four)

Rudolf Steiner spoke these words over eighty years ago at a time when people were just beginning to perceive the complexity of "external life." Now, as we approach the end of the twentieth century, we can witness the acceleration of complexity and the rising tide of discontent. But the dawn of the New Age has made it actually much easier to broach the subject of reincarnation and karma, which has yet to be taken seriously here in the West. The notion of repeated earthly lives has been popularized in fiction, television, comic strips, and even on bumper stickers ("My karma ran over my dogma!"). Such superficial treatment is totally foreign to Steiner's concerns. As spiritual seekers we are called upon to take up matters relating to the life of soul and spirit much more seriously. The questions are more critical than ever. To what extent can the truth of reincarnation and karma actually penetrate modern Western culture? Will people conduct themselves as though they were convinced that they had lived on earth before and that they will be born again into a human body in the future? Such critical issues as birth control, abortion, capital punishment, and euthanasia ignite the hottest political passions, but the debate excludes any mention of karmic consequences. What if poets and priests, scientists and philosophers, artists and doctors were to examine these burning questions in the light of reincarnation and karma? Can we even begin to imagine how the resulting insights would affect the course of human history? Vaclav Havel made a bold beginning.

Anthroposophy teaches that a deepened, Christianized understanding of reincarnation and karma is absolutely essential for the future of civilization and the earth itself. In the fifth lecture of this volume, Rudolf Steiner states:

> The feeling of responsibility will be intensified to a degree that was formerly impossible, and other moral insights will necessarily follow. As human beings learning to live under the influence of the ideas of reincarnation and karma, we shall come to know that our life cannot be assessed on the basis of what has taken expression in one life between birth and death, but that a period extending over many lives must be taken into account.

Steiner further emphasizes that these ideas cannot be taken up superficially; they must be internalized. What is required is the capacity "to penetrate into intimate matters of the life of soul, into things that every soul must experience in the deep foundations of its own core of being." This "intimate" knowledge of the laws operating in the depths of soul is to be gained not through theoretical conceptions, but through one's own inner activity.

The three lectures given in Berlin (lectures one, two, and five) were organized as a series, and several points reappear in the two intervening Stuttgart lectures as well. Students will marvel at Steiner's ability to discuss similar thoughts and illustrations in lively variations. We recognize the same meditation exercises, or "tests" as Steiner calls them, in quite different formulations. We should realize that Steiner is guiding us in the discovery and exploration of genuine soul processes.

The techniques are meant to awaken in each individual the kind of enthusiasm, perceptions, and feelings that become the substance of genuine self-knowledge. Only then can we begin to work in harmony with our higher ego, which passes from one incarnation to the next. Our effort to establish and re-establish that harmony is the essence of karma, and it requires patience and strength. Becoming "sufficiently open" to the mystery of ourselves and the universe demands a unique self-less love, which each of us must nurture if we are to deal with the critical issues of our time and participate in transforming modern life and culture.

HERBERT O. HAGENS
Princeton, New Jersey

Berlin, January 23, 1912

*P*eople who have made some study of anthroposophy, and particularly of the basic principles of reincarnation, karma, and other truths connected with humanity and its evolution, may well ask: Why is it so difficult to gain a true, firsthand conception of that being in humans that passes through repeated earth lives—that being which, if one could only acquire more intimate knowledge of it, would inevitably lead to an insight into the secrets of repeated earth lives and even of karma? It is certainly true to say that as a rule people misinterpret everything connected with this question. At first we try, as is only too natural, to explain it through our ordinary world of thought, through the ordinary intellect, and we ask ourselves: To what extent can we find, in the facts of life, proof that the conception of repeated earth lives and karma is true? This endeavor, which is essentially of the nature of reflection can, admittedly lead us to a certain point, but no further. For our world of thought, as at present constituted, is entirely dependent on those qualities of our human organism that are limited to one incarnation; we possess them because, as human beings living between birth and death, we have been given this particular organism. And on this particular formation of the physical body, with the etheric body which is only one stage higher, everything that we can call our thought world is dependent. The more penetrating these thoughts are, the better able they are to enter into abstract truths—so much the more are they dependent on the outer organism that is limited to one incarnation.

From this we may conclude that when we pass into the life between death and a new birth—that is to say, into the spiritual life—we can take with us least of all what we experience in our souls—our thoughts! And our most penetrating thoughts are what most of all we have to leave behind.

It may be asked: What is it that people especially discard when they pass through the gate of death? First of all, our physical body; and of all that constitutes our inner being we discard practically to the same extent all the abstract thoughts formulated in our soul. These two things—physical body, abstract thoughts, scientific thoughts as well—are what we can least of all take with us when we pass through the gate of death. It is in a certain sense easy to take with us our tempera-ment, our impulses, our desires as they have been formed in us, and especially our habits; we also take with us the mode and nature of our impulses of will—but our thoughts least of all. Therefore, because our thoughts are so intimately bound up with the outer organism, we may conclude that they are instruments not very well adapted to penetrate the secrets of reincarnation and karma, which are truths extending beyond the single incarnation.

All the same, we can reach a certain point, and indeed we must develop our thinking up to a certain point, if we wish to gain insight into the theory of reincarnation and karma. What can be said on this subject has practically all been said either in the pamphlet, *Reincarnation and Karma from the Standpoint of Modern Natural Science*, or in the chapter on reincarnation and karma in the book *Theosophy*. Scarcely anything can be added to what is said in these two publications. The question of what can be contributed by the intellect will not further con-cern us today, but rather the question of how people can acquire a certain conception of reincarnation and karma; that is to say, a conception of more value than a mere theoretical conviction, able to bring about a kind of inner certainty that the real soul-spiritual kernel of being within us comes over from earlier lives and passes on into later lives.

Such a definite conception can be acquired by means of certain inner exercises that are by no means easy; indeed they are difficult, but they can nevertheless be carried out. The first step is in some degree to practice the normal kind of self-cognition which consists in looking back over one's life and asking oneself: What kind of person have I been? Have I been a person with a strong inclination for reflection, for inner contemplation; or am I one who has always had more love for the sensations of the outer world, liking or disliking this or that in everyday life? Was I a child who at school liked reading but not arithmetic, one who liked to hit other children but did not like being hit? Or was I a child always bound to be bullied and not smart enough to bully others?

It is well to look back on one's life in this way, and especially to ask oneself: Was I cut out for activities of the mind or of the will? What did I find easy or difficult? What happened to me that I would like to have avoided? What happenings made me say to myself: "I am glad this has come to pass"—and so on.

It is good to look back on one's life in a certain way, and above all to envisage clearly those things that one did not like. All this leads to a more intimate knowledge of the inner kernel of our being. For example, a son who would have liked to become a poet was destined by his father to be a craftsman, and a craftsman he became, although he would sooner have been a poet. It is well to know clearly what we really wanted to be, and what we have become against our will, to visualize what would have suited us in the time of our youth but was not our lot, and then, again, what we would have liked to avoid.

All that I am saying refers, of course, to life in the past, not in the future—that would be a false conception. We must therefore be quite clear as to what such a retrospect into the past means; it tells us what we did not want, what we would have liked to avoid. When we have made that clear to ourselves, we really have a picture of those things in our life which have pleased us least. That is the essential point. And we must now try to live into a very remarkable conception: we must desire and will everything that we have not desired or willed. We must imagine to ourselves: What should I actually have become if I had ardently desired everything that in fact I did not wish for and which really went against the grain in life? In a certain sense we must here rule out what we have succeeded in overcoming, for the most important thing is that we should ardently wish or picture ourselves wishing for the things we have not desired, or concerning which we have not been able to carry out our wishes, so that we create for ourselves, in feeling and thought, a being hitherto unfamiliar to us. We must picture ourselves as this being with great intensity. If we can do this, if we can identify ourselves with the being we have ourselves built up in this way, we have made some real progress toward becoming acquainted with the inner soul-kernel of our being; for in the picture we have thus been able to make of our own personality there will arise something that we have not been in this present incarnation but which we have introduced into it. Our deeper being will emerge from the picture built up in this way.

You will see, therefore, that from those who wish to gain knowledge of this inner kernel of being, something is required for which people in our age have no inclination at all. They are not disposed to desire anything of the sort, for nowadays, if they reflect upon their own nature, they want to find themselves absolutely satisfied with it as it is. When we go back to earlier, more deeply religious epochs, we find there a feeling that human beings should feel themselves overwhelmed because they so little resembled their divine archetype. This was not, of course, the idea of which we have spoken today, but it was an idea that led people away from what usually satisfies them, to something else, to that being which lives on beyond the organism existing between birth and death, even if it did not lead to the conviction of another incarnation. If you call up the counterpart of yourself, the following thought will dawn upon you. This counterpart—difficult as it may be to realize it as a picture of yourself in this life—is nevertheless connected with you, and you cannot disown it. Once it appears, it will follow you, hover before your soul and crystallize in such a way that you will realize that it has something to do with you, but certainly not with your present life. And then there develops the perception that this picture is derived from an earlier life.

If we bring this clearly before our souls, we shall soon realize how erroneous are most of the current conceptions of reincarnation and karma. You have no doubt often heard anthroposophists say when they meet a good arithmetician: "In a previous incarnation this person was a good arithmetician!" Unfortunately, many undeveloped anthroposophists string together links of reincarnation in such a way that it is thought possible to find the earlier incarnation because the present gifts must have existed in the preceding incarnation or in many previous incarnations. This is the worst possible form of speculation and anything derived from it is usually false. True observation by means of spiritual science discloses, as a rule, the exact opposite. For example, people who in a former incarnation were good arithmeticians, good mathematicians, often reappear with no gift for mathematics at all. If we wish to discover what gifts we may probably have possessed in a former incarnation (here I must remind you that we are speaking of probabilities!)—if we wish to know what intellectual or artistic faculties, say, we possessed in a former incarnation, it is well to reflect upon those things for which we have least talent in the present life.

These are true indications, but they are very often interwoven with other facts. It may happen that someone had a special talent for mathematics in a former incarnation but died young, so that this talent never came to full expression. Then this person will be born again in the next incarnation with a talent for mathematics, and this will represent a continuation of the previous incarnation. Abel, the mathematician who died young, will certainly in his next incarnation be reborn with a strong mathematical talent.[1] But when a mathematician has lived to a great age, so that this talent for mathematics has spent itself— then in the next incarnation that person will be stupid as regards mathematics. I knew a man who had so little gift for mathematics that as a schoolboy he simply hated figures, and although in other subjects he did well, he generally managed to get through his classes only because he obtained exceptionally good marks in other subjects. This was because in his former incarnation he had been an exceedingly good mathematician.

If we go more deeply into this, the fact becomes apparent that a person's external career in one incarnation, when it is not merely a career but also an inner vocation, passes over in the next incarnation into the inward shaping of their bodily organs. Thus, if someone has been an exceptionally good mathematician in one incarnation, the mastery over numbers

---

1. The Norwegian Niels Henrik Abel (1802–1829), of whom Hermite said: "He has left mathematicians something to keep them busy for five hundred years." Two days after Abel's death in poverty, from tuberculosis, a letter came saying that he was to be appointed Professor of Mathematics in the University of Berlin.

and figures remains and goes into a special development of the sense-organs, for instance, of the eyes. People with very good sight have it as a result of the fact that in their former incarnation they thought in forms; they took this thinking in forms with them and during the life between death and rebirth they worked specially on the shaping of their eyes. Here the mathematical talent has passed into the eyes and no longer exists as a gift for mathematics.

Another case known to occultists is where an individuality in one incarnation lived with intensity in architectural forms; these experiences lived as inner soul forces and worked strongly upon the instrument of hearing, so that in the next incarnation the individual became a great musician. This person did not appear as a great architect, because the perception of form necessary for architecture was transformed into an organ-building force, so that there was nothing left but a supreme sensitiveness for music.

An external consideration of similarities is generally deceptive in reference to the characteristics of successive incarnations; and just as we must reflect upon whatever did not please us and conceive of ourselves as having had an intense desire for it, so we must also reflect upon those things for which we have the least talent, and about which we are stupid. If we discover the dullest sides of our nature, they may very probably point to those fields in which we were most brilliant in our previous incarnation. Thus we see how easy it is in these matters to begin at the wrong end. A little reflection will show us that it is the soul-kernel of our being that works over from one incarnation to another; this can be illustrated by the fact that it is no easier for a person to learn a language even if in the preceding incarnation he or she lived in the country associated with this particular language; otherwise our schoolchildren would not find it so difficult to learn Greek and Latin, for many of them in former incarnations will have lived in the regions where these were the languages of ordinary intercourse.

You see, the outer capacities we acquire are so closely connected with earthly circumstances that we cannot speak of them reappearing in the same form in the next incarnation; they are transformed into forces and in that way pass over to a subsequent incarnation. For instance, people who have a special faculty for learning languages in one incarnation will not have this in the next; instead, they will have the faculty that enables them to form more unbiased judgments than those who had less talent for languages; these latter will tend to form one-sided judgments.

These matters are connected with the mysteries of reincarnation, and when we penetrate them we obtain a clear and vivid idea of what truly belongs to our inner being and what must in a certain sense be accounted external. For instance, language today is no longer part of our inner being. We may love a language for the sake of what it expresses, for the sake of its folk spirit; but it is something which passes over in transformed forms of force from one incarnation to another.

If we follow up these ideas, so that we say: "I will strongly desire and will to be what I have become against my will, and also that for which I have the least capacity"—we can know that the conceptions we thus obtain will build up a picture of the preceding incarnation. This picture will arise in great precision if we are earnest and serious about the things just described. It can be observed that from the whole way in which the conceptions coalesce, we will either feel: "This picture is quite near to me," or we will feel: "This picture is a long, long way off."

If through the elaboration of these conceptions such a picture of the previous incarnation arises before our soul, we will, as a rule, be able to estimate how faded the picture is. The following feeling will come as an experience: "I am standing here; but the picture before me could not be my father, my grandfather, or my great-grandfather." If, however, students allow the picture to work upon them, their feeling and perception will lead them to the opinion: "Others are standing between me and this picture." Let us for a moment assume that there is this feeling. It becomes apparent that between me and the picture stand twelve persons; another may perhaps feel there stand seven persons; but in any event the feeling is there and is of the greatest significance. For instance, if there are twelve persons between someone and the picture, this number can be divided by three, and the result will be four, and this may represent the number of centuries that have elapsed since the last incarnation. Thus someone who felt that there were twelve people would say: "My preceding incarnation took place four centuries ago." This is given merely as an example; it will only actually be so in a very few cases, but it conveys the idea. Most people will find that they can in this way rightly estimate when they were incarnated before. Only the preparatory steps, of course, are rather difficult.

Here we have touched upon matters that are as alien as they can possibly be from present-day consciousness, and it cannot be denied that if we spoke of these things to people unprepared for them, they would regard them as so much irresponsible fantasy. The anthroposophical world-picture is fated—more so than any of its predecessors—to oppose traditional, accepted ideas. For to a very great extent these are imbued with the crudest, the most desolate materialism; and those very world-pictures which appear to be most firmly established on a scientific basis have, in point of fact, grown out of the most devastating materialistic assumptions. And since anthroposophy is condemned to be labeled as the outlook cultivated by the kind of person who wants to know about previous incarnations, one can readily understand that people of the present day are very far from taking anthroposophical views seriously. They are as far remote from the inclination to desire and to will what they have never desired or willed, as their habits of thought are remote from spiritual truths. The question might here be asked: Why, then, does spiritual truth come into the world just now? Why does it not leave humanity time to develop, to mature?

The reason is that it is almost impossible to imagine a greater difference between two successive epochs than there will be between the present epoch and that into which humanity will have grown when the people now living are reborn in their next incarnation. The development of certain spiritual faculties does not depend upon humanity, but upon the whole purpose and meaning, the whole nature, of earth evolution. People of the present day could not be more remote than they are from any belief in reincarnation and karma. This does not apply to students of anthroposophy, but they are still very few; neither does it apply to those who still adhere to certain old forms of religion; but it applies to those who are the bearers of external cultural life: it sets them far away from belief in reincarnation and karma. Now the fact that people of the present day are particularly disinclined to believe in reincarnation and karma is connected in a remarkable way with their pursuits and studies—that is, insofar as these concern their intellectual faculties—and this fact will produce the opposite effect in the future. In the next incarnation these people, whether their pursuits are spiritual or material, will have a strong predisposition to gain an impression of their previous incarnation. Quite irrespective of their pursuits in this age, they will be reborn with a strong predisposition, a strong yearning for their last incarnation, with a strong desire to experience and know something of it. We are standing at a turning point in time; it will lead people from an incarnation in which they have no desire at all to know anything of reincarnation and karma, to one in which the most living feeling will be this: "The whole of the life I now lead has no foundation for me if I cannot know anything of my former incarnation." And the very people who now inveigh most bitterly against reincarnation and karma will writhe under the torment of the next life because they cannot explain to themselves how their life has come to be what it is.

Anthroposophy is not here for the purpose of cultivating in us a retrospective longing for former lives, but in order that there should be understanding of what will arise in connection with collective humanity when the people who are alive today will be here again. People who are anthroposophists today will share the desire to remember with those who are not , but they will have understanding, and therefore an inner harmony in their soul life. Those who reject anthroposophy today will wish to know something of it in the next life; they will really feel something like an inner torment concerning their previous incarnation but they will understand nothing of what it is that most distresses and torments them; they will be perplexed and will lack inner harmony. In their next incarnation they will have to be told: "You will understand the cause of this torment only if you can conceive that you have actually willed it into existence." Naturally, nobody will desire this torment, but people who are materialists today will in their next incarnation begin to understand their inner demands and the advice of those who will be in a position to know and who may say to them: "Conceive to yourselves that you have willed into existence this life from which you would like to flee." If they begin to follow this advice and reflect: "How can I have willed this life?" they will say to themselves: "Yes, I did perhaps live in an incarnation where I said that it was absurdity and nonsense to speak of a following incarnation, and that this life was complete in itself, sending no forces on into a later one. And because at that time I felt a future life to be unreal, to be non-sense, my life now is so empty and desolate. It was I who actually implanted within myself the thought that is now the force making my life so meaningless and barren."

That will be a right thought. Karmically it will outlive materialism. The next incarnation will be full of meaning for those who have acquired the conviction that their life, as it now is, is not only complete in itself but contains causes for the next. Meaningless and desolate will be the life of those who, because they believe reincarnation to be nonsense, have themselves rendered their own lives barren and void.

So we see that the thoughts we cherish do not pass over into the next life in a somewhat intensified form, but arise there transformed into forces. In the spiritual world, thoughts such as we now form between birth and death have no significance except insofar as they are transformed. If, for instance, we have a great thought, however great it may be, the thought as thought is gone when we pass through the gate of death, but the enthusiasm, the perception and the feeling called to life by the thought—these pass through the gate of death with us. We do not even take with us the thoughts of anthroposophy, but what we have experienced through them—even to the details, not the general fundamental feeling alone—that is taken with us. This in particular is the point to grasp; thoughts as such are of real significance for the physical plane, but when we are speaking of the activity of thoughts in the higher worlds we must at the same time speak of their transformation in confor-mity with those worlds. Thoughts that deny reincarnation are transformed in the next life into an inner unreality, an inner emptiness of life; this inner unreality and emptiness are experi-enced as torment, as disharmony.

With the aid of a simile we may obtain an idea of this by thinking of something we like very much, and are always glad to see in a certain place—for instance, a particular flower blooming in a certain spot. If the flower is cut by a ruthless hand, we experience a certain pain. So it is with the whole human organism. What causes the human being to feel pain? When the etheric and astral elements of an organ are embedded in a particular position in the physical body, then if the organ is injured so that the etheric and astral bodies cannot permeate it properly, pain is the result. It is just like the ruthless cutting of a rose from its accustomed place in a garden. When an organ has been injured, the etheric and astral bodies do not find what they seek, and this is then felt as bodily pain. And so a our own thoughts, working on into the future, will meet us in the future. If we send over into the next incarnation no forces of faith or of knowledge, our thoughts will fail us, and when we seek for them we will find nothing. This lack will be experienced as pain and torment.

These are matters which from one aspect make the karmic course of certain events clear to us. They must be made clear, for our aim is to penetrate still more deeply into the ways and means whereby we can make yet further preparation for coming to know the real kernel of our being of spirit and soul.

*T*he thoughts contained in the last lecture will have seemed incomprehensible to many of you in that form, perhaps they were even matters of doubt; but if we go further into the subject today they will become clearer.

What was it that was presented to us in the last lectures? For the whole of our being it was somewhat similar to what people accomplish when they are in some position in life where they have to reflect upon earlier occurrences and experiences, and call them back into memory. Memory and remembrance are experiences of the human soul which, in ordinary consciousness, are really connected only with the course of the soul's life between birth and death—or more exactly, with the period of time that begins in the later years of childhood and last until death.

We know that in ordinary consciousness our memory goes back only to a definite point of time in our childhood, and we have to be told about earlier events by our parents, elder relations, or friends. When we consider this stretch of time, we speak of it in relation to the soul life as "remembered." It is not, of course, possible here to go more deeply into the meaning of the words "power of remembering" or "memory," nor is it necessary for our purpose. We need only bring clearly before our souls that everything designated by these words is bound up with reflecting on past events or experiences. What we spoke of in the last lecture is akin to this reflecting, but it must not be equated with ordinary memory; it should be regarded rather as a higher, wider power of memory that leads us beyond this present incarnation to a sense of certainty that we have had previous earth lives.

If we picture someone who needs to recall something that was learned at an early period of life, and attunes their soul to bring out of the depths what was learned then in order to follow it through in the present—if we form a living conception of this process of recollection, we see in it a function that belongs to our ordinary faculty of remembrance. In the last lecture we were speaking of functions of the soul, but those functions ought to lead to something that arises in our inner being in relation to our earlier earth life, similar to that which arises in our souls in this life when we feel a past experience springing up in memory. Therefore you must not regard what was said in the last lecture as though this were all that is needed to lead us to an earlier earth life, nor as though it were able immediately to evoke a right conception of the kind of people we were in an earlier incarnation. It is only an aid, just as self-recollection is an aid, helping us to draw forth what has disappeared into the background of the soul's life. Let us briefly sum up what we have grasped concerning such a recollection in reference to a former earth life. This can best be done in the following way: A little self-knowledge will render many of life's happenings comprehensible to us. If something disagreeable happens and we do not fully see the reason for it, we may say to ourselves: "I really am a careless person, and it is no wonder this happened to me." This shows at least some understanding of what has happened. There are, however, countless experiences in life of which we simply cannot conceive that they are connected with the forces and faculties of our soul. In ordinary life we usually speak of them as "accidental." We speak of "accidents" when we do not perceive how the things that befall us as strokes of fate are connected with the inner leanings of our soul, and so forth. In the last lecture attention was drawn also to events of another kind—experiences through which in a sense we extricate ourselves, by means of what we generally call our Ego, from some situation we are in. For example: we may be destined by our parents or near relations to a certain calling or position in life, and we feel we must at all costs leave it and do something else. When in later life we look back on something like this, we say to ourselves: "We were put into a certain position in life, but by our own impulse of will, by our personal sympathy or antipathy, we have extricated ourselves from it."

The point is not to pay attention to all manner of things, but to confine ourselves in our retrospective memory to something that vitally affected our life. If, for instance, a man has never felt any desire, nor had any motive to become a sailor, a will-impulse such as was referred to in the last lecture does not come into consideration at all, but only one whereby he actually brought about a change of fate, a reversal of some situation in life. But when in later life we remember something of this kind and realize that we extricated ourselves, we should not cultivate any rueful feelings about it, as though we ought to have stayed where we were. The essential point is not the practical outcome of the decision, but the recollection of when such turning points occurred. Then with regard to events of which we say, "This happened by chance," or "We were in such and such a position but have extricated ourselves from it," we must evoke with utmost energy the following inner experience.

We say to ourselves: "I will imagine that the position from which I extricated myself was one in which I deliberately placed myself with the strongest impulse of will." We bring before our own souls the very thing that was repugnant to us and from which we extricated ourselves. We do this in such a way that we say: "As an experiment I will give myself up to the idea that I willed this with all my might; I will bring before my soul the picture of someone who willed something like this with all their might." And let us imagine that we ourselves brought about the events called "accidents." Suppose it has come back to our memory that at some place a stone fell from a building onto our shoulders and hurt us badly. Then let us imagine that we had climbed onto the roof and placed the stone so that it was bound to fall, and that then we ran quickly under it so that it had to fall on us. It is of no consequence that such ideas are grotesque; the point is what we want to acquire through them.

Let us now put ourselves right into the soul of the person of whom we have built up such a picture, the person who has actually willed everything that has happened to us "by accident," who has desired everything from which we have extricated ourselves. There will be no result in the soul if we practice such an exercise two or three or four times only, but a great deal will result if we practice it in connection with the innumerable experiences which we shall find if we look for them. If we do this over and over again, forming a living conception of the person who has willed everything that we have not willed we shall find that the picture never leaves us again, that it makes a very remarkable impression on us, as though it really had something to do with us. If we then acquire a certain delicate perception in this kind of self-probation, we shall soon discover how such a mood and such a picture, built up by ourselves, resemble an image we have called up from memory. The difference is only this, that when we call up such an image from memory in the ordinary way, it generally remains simply an image, but when we practice the exercises of which we have been speaking, what comes to life in the soul has in it an element of feeling, an element connected more with the moods of the soul, and less with images. We feel a particular relationship to this picture. The picture itself is not of much account, but the feelings we have make an impression similar to that made by memory-images. If we repeat this process over and over again, we arrive through an inner clarification at the "knowledge," one might say, that the picture we have built up is becoming clearer and clearer, just as a memory-image does when one starts to recall it out of dark depths of the soul.

Thus it is not a question of what we imagine, for this changes and becomes something different. It goes through a process similar to that which occurs when we want to remember a particular name and it nearly comes and then goes: we have a partial recollection of it and then say, for instance, Nuszbaumer. Then, without our being able to say why, the right name comes to us—Nuszdorfer, perhaps. Just as here the names Nuszbaumer, Nuszdorfer, build each other up, so the picture rights itself and changes. This is what causes the feeling to arise: "Here I have attained something that exists within me, and by the way it exists within me and is related to the rest of my soul life, it plainly shows me that it cannot have existed within me in this form in my present incarnation!" So we perceive with the greatest inner clarity that what exists within us in this form, lies further back. Only we must realize that we are here dealing with a kind of faculty of remembrance which can be developed in the human soul, a faculty which, in contradistinction to the ordinary faculty of remembrance, must be designated by a different name. We must designate the ordinary faculty of remembrance as "image-memory," but the faculty of remembrance now in question must really be described as a kind of "feeling and experience memory." That this has a certain foundation can be proved by the following reflections.

We must bear in mind that our ordinary faculty of remembrance is really a kind of image-memory. Think how a specially painful event that perhaps happened to you twenty years ago, reappears in memory. The event may come up before you in all its details, but the pain you suffered is no longer felt to the same extent; it is in a sense blotted out of the memory-image. There are, of course different degrees, and it may well happen that something has struck us such a blow that again and again a fresh and more intense sorrow is felt when we remember the experience. The general principle, however, holds good: so far as our present incarnation is concerned our faculty of remembrance is an image-memory, whereas the feelings that were experienced, or the will-impulses themselves, do not arise again in the soul with anything like the same intensity.

We need only take a characteristic example and we shall see how great the difference is between the image that arises in the memory, and what has remained of feelings and will-impulses. Let us think of a man who writes his memoirs. Suppose, for example, that Bismarck, in writing his memoirs, has come to the point when he prepared for the German-Austrian War of 1866, and imagine what may have taken place in his soul at that highly critical point, when he led and guided events against a host of condemnations and will-impulses. Do not conceive how all this lived in his soul at that time, but imagine that all he then experienced under the immediate impression of the events sank down into the depths of his soul; then imagine how faded the feelings and will-impulses must have become by the time he wrote his memoirs compared with what they were when he was actually carrying out the project. Nobody can fail to realize what a difference there is between the memory-image and the original feelings and will-impulses involved.

Those who have gone a little way into anthroposophy will understand what has often been said: that our conceptual activity—including the conceptual activity related to memory—is something which, when roused by the external world in which we live in our physical bodies, has meaning only for this single incarnation. The fundamental principles of anthroposophy have always taught us the great truth that all the concepts and ideas we make our own when we perceive anything through the senses, when we fear or hope for anything in life—this does not relate to impulses of the soul, but to concepts—all that makes up our conceptual life disappears very soon after we have passed through the gate of death. For concepts belong to the things that pass away with physical life, to the things that are least enduring. Anyone, however, who has given any study to the laws of reincarnation and karma can readily understand that our concepts, as we acquire them in the life that flows on in relation to the outer world or to the things of the physical plane, come to expression in speech, and that we can therefore in a sense connect the conceptual life with speech. Now we all know that we have to learn to speak some particular language in a given incarnation; for while it is obvious that many modern schoolchildren incarnated in ancient Greece, none of them find it easier to learn Greek by being able to remember how they spoke Greek in a previous incarnation! Speech is entirely an expression of our conceptual life, and their fates are similar; so that concepts drawn from the physical world, and even the concepts we must acquire about the higher worlds, are in a sense always colored by subjective pictures of the external world. Only when we have insight do we realize what concepts are able to tell about the higher worlds. What we learn directly from concepts is also, in a sense, bound up with life between birth and death. After death we do not form concepts as we form them here; after death we see them, they are objects of perception; they exist just as colors and tones exist in the physical world. In the physical world what we picture to ourselves by means of conceptions carries an impress of physical matter, but in the disembodied state we have concepts before us in the same way as here we have colors and tones. We cannot, of course, see red or blue as we see them here with our physical eyes, but what we do not see here, and about which we form concepts, is the same for us after death as red, green, or any other color or sound is here. What we learn to know in the physical world purely through concepts, or rather ideas (in the sense of *The Philosophy of Spiritual Activity*) can be seen only through the veil of the conceptual life, but in the disembodied state it stands there in the way that the physical world stands before our consciousness. In the physical world there are people who really think that sense impressions yield everything. What we can make clear to ourselves by means of a concept—as for instance the concept "lamb" or "wolf"—embraces everything the senses give us; but that which transcends matter can actually be denied by those who admit the existence of the sense-impression only. We can make a mental picture of all we see as lamb or wolf. Now the ordinary outlook tries to suggest that what can here be built up in a conceptual sense is nothing more than a "mere idea." But if we were to shut up a wolf and for a long time feed him on nothing else but lamb, so that he is filled with nothing but lamb-substance—nobody could possibly persuade themselves that the "wolf" has thereby become "lamb." Therefore we must say: obviously, here, what transcends a sense impression is a concept. Certainly, there is no denying that what bodies forth the concept, dies; but what lives in "wolf," what lives in "lamb"—what is within them and cannot be seen by the physical eyes—this is "seen," perceived, in the life between death and rebirth.

Thus when it is said that conceptions are bound up with the physical body, we must not infer that humanity will be without conceptions, or rather without the content of the conceptions in the life between death and rebirth. Only that which has worked out the conceptions, disappears. Our conceptual life, as we experience it here in the physical world, has significance only for the life of this incarnation. In this connection I have already mentioned the case of Friedrich Hebbel, who once sketched out in his diary an ingenious plan for a drama. He had the idea of the reincarnated Plato in a school class, making the worst possible impression on the teacher and being severely reprimanded because he could not understand Plato! Here, too, is a suggestion that Plato's thought structure—all that lived in him as thought—does not survive in the same form in his next incarnation.

In order to obtain a reasonable view of these things, we must consider the soul life of the human being from a certain point of view. We must ask ourselves: What do we carry about as the content of our soul life? First, we have our concepts. The fact that these concepts, permeated with feeling, can lead to impulses of will, does not prevent us from speaking of a specific life of concepts in the soul. For although there are people who can hardly confine themselves to a pure concept but immediately they conceive anything flare up in sympathy or antipathy, thus passing over into other impulses, this does not mean that the life of concepts cannot be separated from other contents of the soul.

Secondly, we have in our soul life experiences of feeling. These appear in a great diversity of forms. There are the well-known antitheses in the life of feeling which can be spoken of as the sympathy and the antipathy we feel for things, or, if we want to describe them more emphatically, as love and hate. We can say that these feelings produce a kind of stimulus, and again there are feelings that bring about a certain tension and release. They cannot be classed with sympathy and antipathy. For a soul impulse that can be described as a tension, a stimulus, or as a release, is different from what comes to expression in mere sympathy or antipathy. We should have to talk for a long time if it were a question of describing all the different kinds of feelings. To these also belong what may be described as the sense for beauty and for ugliness, which is a specific soul content and does not resemble feelings of sympathy and antipathy. At all events it cannot be classed with them. We could also describe the specific feelings we have for good or evil. This is not the time to enlarge upon the difference between our inner experiences regarding a good or evil action, and the feelings of sympathy or antipathy for such actions— our love of a good action and hatred of an evil one. Thus we meet with feelings in the most diverse forms and we can distinguish them from our concepts.

A third kind of soul experiences are the impulses of will, the life of will. This again must not be classed with what may be called experiences of feeling, which can or must remain enclosed within our soul life, according to the way we experience them. An impulse of will says: "You shall do this, you shall do that." For we must distinguish between the mere feeling we have of what seems good or evil to ourselves or to others, and what arises in the soul as more than a feeling when we are impelled to do good and to refrain from evil. Judgment can remain rooted in feeling but the impulses of will are a different matter. Although there are transitions between the life of feeling and the impulses of will, we ought not on the basis of ordinary observation to class them together without further consideration. In human life there are transitions everywhere. Just as there are people who never arrive at pure conceptions but always express simultaneously their love or hatred, who are thrown hither and thither because they cannot separate their feelings from their conceptions, so there are others who, when they see something, cannot refrain from going on, through an impulse of will, to an action, even if the action is unjustifiable. This leads to no good. It takes the form of kleptomania and so forth. Here there is no ordered relationship between the feelings and the impulses of the will, although in reality a sharp distinction should be drawn between them.

Thus in our life of soul we live in ideas, in feelings, and in impulses of will. We have seen that the life of ideas is connected with a single incarnation between birth and death; we have seen how we enter life and build up our own life of ideas. This is not the case with the life of feeling, or with the life of will. Of those who insist that it is, one can only think that they can never have observed intelligently the development of a child. Consider a child in relation to the life of ideas before it can speak; it relates itself to the surrounding world through its conceptions or ideas. But it has very decided sympathies and antipathies, and active impulses of will for or against something. The decisiveness of these early will-impulses has actually misled a philosopher— Schopenhauer—into the belief that a person's character cannot be altered at all during life. This is not correct; the character can be altered. We must realize that when we enter physical life the position as regards the feelings and the impulses of will is in no way the same as it is regarding the life of concepts, for we enter an incarnation with a very definite equipment of feeling experiences and impulses of will. Correct observation might indeed make us surmise that in the feelings and will-impulses we have something that we have brought with us from earlier incarnations. And all this must be brought together as a "feeling-memory" in contradistinction to the "concept-memory" that belongs to one life only. We can arrive at no practical result if we take into account only a concept-memory. All that we develop in the life of concepts cannot call forth an impression which, if rightly understood, says to us: You have within you something that entered this incarnation with you at birth. For this we must go beyond the life of concepts; recollection must become something different, and we have shown what recollection can indeed become. How do we practice self-recollection? We do not merely picture to ourselves: "This was accidental in our life, such and such a thing befell us, there we were in a position of life which we abandoned," and so forth. We must not stop at the concepts; we must make them living, active, as if there stood before us the picture of a personality who had desired and willed all this. We must experience ourselves in this willing. This is a very different experience from that of merely recalling concepts; it is an experience of living oneself into other soul forces, if I may put it in that way.

This practice of drawing on will and desire in order to fill the soul with a certain content—a practice that has always been known and cultivated in all occult schools—is confirmed by what we know from anthroposophical or similar knowledge of the life of thinking, feeling, and willing, and can be understood and explained thereby. Let us be quite clear that in giving a specific content to the life of feeling and will we must develop something that resembles memory-concepts, but does not stop there. It is something that enables us to develop another kind of memory—one that gradually leads us beyond the life enclosed in one incarnation between birth and death.

It must be strongly emphasized that the path here indicated is absolutely good and sure—but full of renunciation. It is easier to imagine on all sorts of external grounds that one has been Marie Antoinette or Mary Magdalene, or somebody like that in a former incarnation. It is more difficult by the methods described to construct out of what actually exists in the soul a picture of what one really was. For this reason we have to renounce a good deal, for we can readily be deceived. If someone says: "Yes, and it is also quite possible to imagine something in relation to our memories that never existed," all these things are no real objections. Life itself can provide a criterion for distinguishing real imagination from fancy.

Somebody once said to me in a town in South Germany that everything in my book *Occult Science* might be based on simple suggestion. He said suggestion could be so vivid that one could even imagine lemonade so strongly that the taste of it would be in the mouth; and if such a thing is possible, why should it not be possible for what is present in *Occult Science* to be based on suggestion? Theoretically such an objection may be raised, but life brings the reflection that if anyone wishes to show by the example of lemonade how strongly suggestion can work, we must add that they have not understood how to carry the idea to its logical conclusion. They ought to try not only to imagine lemonade, but to quench their thirst with purely imaginary lemonade. Then they would see that it cannot be done. It is always necessary to carry our experiences to their conclusion, and this cannot be done theoretically but only by direct experience. With the same certainty by which we know that what arises from our memory-concepts is something we have experienced, so do the impulses of will we have called forth with regard to the accidents and undesired happenings arise from the depths of the soul as a picture of earlier experiences. We cannot disprove the statement of anyone who says: "That may be imagination," any more than we can disprove theoretically what numerous people imagine they have experienced and quite certainly have not, nor prove to them what it is they really experienced. No theoretical proof is possible in either case.

We have shown in this way how earlier experience shines into present experiences, and how through careful soul development we really can create for ourselves the conviction—

not only a theoretical conviction but a practical conviction—that our soul reincarnates; we come to know that it has existed before. There are, however, experiences of a very different kind in our lives—experiences of which, when we recall them in memory, we must say: "In the form in which they appear, they do not explain an earlier life to us." Today I shall give an example of only one kind of such experiences, although the same thing may happen in a hundred, in a thousand, different ways.

A woman may be walking in a wood, and being lost in thought may forget that the woodland path ends within a few steps at a precipice. Absorbed in her problem, she walks on at such a pace that in two or three steps more it will be impossible for her to stop and she will fall over to her death. But just as she is on the verge, she hears a voice say, "Stop!" The voice makes such an impression upon her that she stops as though nailed to the spot. She thinks there must be someone who has saved her. She realizes that her life would have been at an end if she had not been pulled up in this way. She looks around—and sees nobody.

The materialistic thinker will say that owing to some circumstance or other an auditory hallucination had come from the depths of the woman's soul, and it was a happy chance that she was saved in this way. But there may be other ways of looking at the event; that at least should be admitted. I only mention this today, for these "other ways" can only be told, not proved. We may say: "Processes in the spiritual world have brought it about that at the moment when you reached your karmic crisis, your life was bestowed on you as a gift. If things had gone further without this occurrence, your life would have been at an end; it is now as though a gift was given to you, and you owe this new life to the powers who stand behind the voice."

Many people of the present time might have such experiences if they would only practice real self-knowledge. Such occurrences happen in the lives of many, many people in the present age. It is not that they do not happen, but that people do not pay attention to them, for such things do not always happen so decisively as in the example given; with their habitual lack of attention, people overlook them. The following is a characteristic example of how unobservant people are of what happens around them.

I knew a school inspector in a country where a law was passed to the effect that the older teachers, who had not obtained certain certificates, were to be examined. Now this school inspector was an extremely human person, and he said to himself: "The young teachers fresh from college can be asked any question, but it would be cruel to ask the older teachers who have been in office for twenty or thirty years the same questions. I had better question them about the contents of the books from which they have taught the children year after year." And lo!—most of the teachers knew nothing of what they themselves had been teaching to their pupils. Yet this man was an examiner who understood how to draw out of people what they knew.

This is only one example of how unobservant people are of what takes place around them, even when it concerns their own affairs. We need not then be surprised that things of this kind happen to many people in life, for only by a true, deliberate self-perception do they come to light. If we bring the proper devout attitude to bear on such an event we may experience a very definite feeling—the feeling that from the day our life was given to us as a gift, its course from then onward must assume a special direction. That is a good feeling, and works like a memory process when we say to ourselves: "I had reached a karmic crisis; there my life ended." If we steep ourselves in this devout feeling, we may experience something that makes us realize: "This is not a memory-concept such as I have often experienced in life—it is something of a very special nature."

In the next lecture I shall be able to speak more fully of what can only be indicated today; for this is how a great initiate of modern times tests those whom he thinks fit to be his followers. For the events that are to take us into the spiritual world proceed from spiritual facts that happen around us, or from a right understanding of them. And such a voice, calling as it does to many people, is not to be regarded as a hallucination; for through such a voice the leader whom we call by the name of Christian Rosenkreuz speaks to those whom he chooses from among the multitude to be his followers. The call proceeds from that individuality who lived in a special incarnation in the thirteenth century. So that those who have an experience of this kind have a sign, a token of recognition, through which they can enter the spiritual world.[1]

There may not be many as yet able to recognize this call, but anthroposophy will work in such a way that, if not in this incarnation, later on people will give heed to it. With most people who have such an experience today it is not completed in the sense that one can say of them in this incarnation: "They have met the initiate who has appointed them his own." One could say it rather of their life between their last death and their present birth. This is an indication that something happens in the life between death and rebirth; that we experience there important events—perhaps more important than in our life here between birth and death. It may happen, and in individual cases it does, that certain persons now belonging to

---

1. See the volume entitled *Christian Rosenkreuz*. Notes of lectures given during the years 1911 and 1912.

Christian Rosenkreuz came to him in a former incarnation, but for most people the destiny that is reflected in such an event occurred in their last life between death and rebirth.

I am not saying this to recount something sensational, nor even for the sake of relating this particular occurrence, but for a special reason; and I should like to add something else in this connection, from an experience I have often had in our movement. I have often found that things I have said are easily forgotten, or retained in a different form from that in which they were said. For this reason I sometimes emphasize important and essential things several times over, not in order to repeat myself. Therefore today I repeat that there are many people at the present time who have passed through an experience such as has been described. The point is not that the experience is not there, but that it is not remembered, because proper attention has not been paid to it. Therefore this should be a consolation to those who say to themselves: "I find nothing of the kind, so I do not belong to those who have been chosen in this way." They can have the assurance that there are countless people at the present time who have experienced something of the kind—I reaffirm this only in order that the real reason for saying these things may be understood.

Such things are told in order to draw our attention again and again to the fact that in a concrete sense, and not through abstract theories, we must find the relation of our soul life to the spiritual worlds. Anthroposophical spiritual science should be for us not merely a theoretical conception of the world, but an inner life force; we should not merely know, "There is a spiritual world to which humanity belongs," but as we go through life we should not only take account of things that stimulate our thinking through the senses, but should grasp with comprehension the connections that show us: "I have my place in the spiritual world, a definite place." The real, concrete place of the individual in the spiritual world—that is the essential point to which we are calling attention.

In a theoretical sense people try to establish that the world may have a spiritual element, and that the human being is not to be considered in a materialistic sense, but may have an inner spiritual element. Our particular conception of the world differs from this, for it says to the individual: "This is your special connection with the spiritual world." More and more we shall be able to ascend to those things that can show us how we must view the world in order to perceive our connection with the spirit of the great world, the macrocosm.

Stuttgart, February 20, 1912

When we observe how life takes its course around us, how it throws its waves into our inner life, into everything we are destined to feel, to suffer, or to delight in during our present existence on the earth, we can think of several groups or kinds of experiences.

As regards our own faculties and talents, we find to begin with that when we succeed in something or other, we may say: being what we are, it is quite natural and understandable that we should succeed in this or that case. But certain failures, perhaps just those that must be called misfortune and calamity, may also become intelligible when viewed in the whole setting of our nature.

In such cases we may not, perhaps, always be able to prove exactly how this or that failure is connected with our own shortcomings in one direction or another. But when we are obliged to say of ourselves in a general way: In many respects you were a superficial character in your present life, so it is understandable that in certain circumstances you were bound to fail—then we may not immediately perceive the connection between the failure and the shortcomings, but generally speaking we shall realize that if we have been frivolous and superficial, success cannot always be at our fingertips.

From what has been said you may think that some kind of causal connection could have been evident between what inevitably happened and your faculties or incompetencies. But there are many things in life where, however conscientiously we set to work, we are not able at once to connect success or failure with these faculties or shortcomings; how we ourselves were at fault or why we deserved success remains a mystery. In short, when thinking more of our inner life we shall be able to distinguish two groups of experiences: in the case of the one group we are aware of the causes of our successes and failures; in the case of the second group we shall not be able to detect any such connection, and that we failed in one particular instance and succeeded in another will seem to be more or less chance. To begin with, we will bear in mind that there is ample evidence in life of this latter group of facts and experiences, and will return to it later.

In contrast to what has just been said, we can think more about our destiny in outer life. There again, two groups of facts will have to be kept in mind. There are cases where it is inwardly clear to us that in connection with events that befall us—not, therefore, those we ourselves initiated—we did certain things and consequently are to blame for these happenings. But of another group of experiences we shall be very liable to say that we can see no connection whatever with what we resolved, what we intended. These are events of which it is usually said that they broke in upon our life as if by chance; they seem to have no connection whatever with anything we ourselves have brought about.

It is this second group of experiences in their relation to our inner life that we shall now consider, that is to say, those happenings where we are unable to perceive any direct or immediate connection with our faculties and shortcomings—outer events, therefore, which we call chance events, of which we cannot at the outset perceive how they could have been brought about by any preceding factor. By way of test, a kind of experiment can be made with these two groups of experiences. The experiment entails no obligations; it is a question merely of putting to the test what will now be characterized.

The experiment can take the following form. We ask ourselves: How would it be if we were to build up in thought a kind of imaginary human being, saying of that person just those things between which we can see no connection by means of our own faculties; we endow this imaginary person with the qualities and faculties that have led, in our own case, to these incomprehensible happenings. We there imagine someone possessing faculties of such a kind that he or she will inevitably succeed or fail in matters where we cannot say the same in connection with our own shortcomings or faculties. We imagine this person as one who has quite deliberately brought about the events that seem to have come into our life by chance.

Simple examples can serve as the starting point here. Suppose a tile from a roof has fallen upon and injured our shoulders. We shall be inclined to attribute this to chance. But to begin with as an experiment, we now build up in thought an imaginary person who acts in the following strange way. This individual climbs on a roof, quickly loosens a tile, but only to the point where it still has a certain hold; then runs quickly to the ground so that when the tile has become quite detached, it falls on this person's shoulders. The same can be done in the case of all events that seem to have come into our life by chance. We build up an imaginary person who is guilty of or brings about all those things of which in ordinary life we cannot see how they are connected with us.

Such a procedure may seem at first to be nothing but a play of fancy. No obligation is incurred by it, but one remarkable thing emerges. When we have imagined such a person with the qualities referred to, it makes a very memorable impression upon us. We cannot get rid of the picture we have thus created in thought; although the picture seems so artificial, it fascinates us, gives the impression that it must, after all, have something to do with ourselves. The feeling we have of this imaginary thought-person accounts for this. If we steep ourselves in this picture it will most certainly not leave us free. A remarkable process then takes shape within our soul, an inner process that is enacted in human beings all the time. We may think of something, make a resolution; for this we need something we once knew, and we use all sorts of artificial means for recalling it. This effort to call up into memory something that has escaped us is, of course, a process in the life of the soul—"recollection" as it is usually called. All the thoughts we summon up to help us to remember something are auxiliary thoughts. Just try for once to realize how many and how often such thoughts have to be used and dropped again, in order to get at what we want to know. The purpose of these auxiliary thoughts is to open the way to the recollection needed at the moment.

In exactly the same, but in a far more comprehensive sense, the "thought-person" described represents an auxiliary process. Such a person never leaves us alone; but is astir in us in such a way that we realize: this person lives in us as a thought, as something that goes on working, that is actually transformed within us into the idea, the thought, which now flashes up suddenly into our soul in the ordinary process of recollection; it is something that overwhelms us. It is as though something says to us: This being cannot remain as it is, it transforms something within you, it becomes alive, it changes! This forces itself upon us in such a way that the imaginary person whispers to us: This is something that has to do with another earth existence, not with the present one. A kind of recollection of another earth existence—that is the thought which quite definitely arises. It is really more a feeling than a thought, a sentient experience, but of such a kind that we feel as though what arises in the soul is what we ourselves once were in an earlier incarnation on this earth.

Anthroposophy regarded in its entirety is by no means merely a sum-total of theories, of presentations of facts, but it gives us directives and indications for achieving our aspirations. Anthroposophy says: If you carry out certain exercises you will be led nearer to the point where recollection is easier for you. It can also be said—and this is drawn from the sphere of actual experience: If you adopt this procedure you get an inner impression, a sentient impression, of the person you were in an earlier life. We there achieve what may be called an extension of memory. What discloses itself to us is, to begin with, a thought reality only, as long as we are building up the imaginary person described. But this imaginary person does not remain a thought being. Through inner transformation, this person becomes sentient impressions, impressions in the life of soul, and while this is going on we realize that this experience has something to do with our earlier incarnation. Our memory extends to this earlier incarnation.

In this present incarnation we remember those things in which our thoughts participated. But in ordinary life, what has played into our life of feeling does not so easily remain vivid and alive. If you try to think back to something that caused you great pain ten or twenty years ago, you will be able to recall the mental picture of it without difficulty; you will be able to cast your thoughts back to what then took place; but you cannot recapture the actual, immediate experience of the pain felt at the time. The pain fades, the remembrance of it streams into the life of ideation. What has here been described is a memory in the soul, a memory belonging to the life of feeling. And as such we actually feel our earlier incarnation. There does, in fact, arise what may be called a remembrance of earlier incarnations. It is not possible immediately to perceive what is playing over into the present incarnation, what is actually the bearer of the remembrance of earlier incarnations. Consider how intimately our thoughts are united with what gives expression to them, with our speech and language. Language is the embodiment of the world of thoughts and ideas. In each life, every human being has to learn the language anew. A child of the very greatest philologist or linguist has to learn the mother tongue by dint of effort. There has yet to be a case of a grammar school child learning Greek with ease because the Greek they had spoken in earlier incarnations was rapidly remembered!

The poet Hebbel jotted down one or two thoughts for the plan of a drama he intended to write. It is a pity that he did not actually carry out this project, for it would have been an extremely interesting drama. The theme was to have been that Plato, reincarnated as a schoolboy, received the very lowest marks for his understanding of the Plato of old! We need not remind ourselves that some teachers are severe, or pedantic. We realize that what Hebbel jotted down is due to the fact that the element of thought, which is also in play in the mental pictures of immediate experiences, is limited more or less to the present incarnation. As we have now heard, the first impression of the earlier incarnation comes as a direct memory in the life of feeling, as a new kind of memory. The impression we get when this memory arises from the imaginary person we have created in thought is more like a feeling, but of such a kind that we realize: the impression comes from some being who once existed and who you yourself were. Something that is like a feeling arising in an act of remembrance is what comes to us as a first impression of the earlier incarnation.

The creation of an imaginary person in thought is simply a means of proving to us that this means is something that transforms itself into an impression in the life of soul, or the life of feeling. Everyone who comes to anthroposophy has the opportunity of carrying out what has now been described. And if people do so they will actually receive an inner impression of which—to use a different illustration—they might speak as follows: "I once saw a landscape; I have forgotten what it actually looked like, but I know it delighted me!" If this happened during the present life, the landscape will no longer make a very vivid impression of feeling; but if the impression of the landscape came from an earlier incarnation the impression will be particularly vivid. In the form of a feeling we can obtain a very vivid impression of our earlier incarnation. And if we then observe such impressions objectively, we may at times experience something like a feeling of bitterness, bittersweetness or acidity from what emerges as the transformation of the imaginary thought-person. This bittersweet or some such feeling is the impression made upon us by our earlier incarnation; it is an impression of feeling, an impression in the life of soul.

The endeavor has now been made to draw attention to something that can ultimately promote in every human being a kind of certainty of having existed in an earlier life—certainty through having engendered a feeling of inner impressions which we know were most definitely not received in this present life. Such an impression, however, arises in the same way as a recollection arises in ordinary life. We may now ask: "How can one know that the impression is actually a recollection?" There it can only be said that to "prove" such a thing is not possible. But the process is the same as it is elsewhere in life when we remember something and are in a sound state of mind. We know there that what arises within us in thought is actually related to something we have experienced. The experience itself gives the certainty. What we picture in the way indicated gives us the certainty that the impression which arises in the soul is not related to anything that had to do with us in the present life but to something in the earlier life.

We have there called forth in ourselves by artificial means, something that brings us into connection with our earlier life. We can also use many different kinds of experiences as tests, and eventually awaken in ourselves feelings of earlier lives.

Here again, from a different aspect, the experiences we have in life can be divided into groups. In the one group may be included the sufferings, sorrows, and obstacles we have encountered; in a second group may be included the joys, happinesses, and advantages in our life. Again as a test, we can take the following standpoint, and say: Yes, we have had these sorrows, these sufferings. Being what we are in this incarnation, with normal life running its course, our sorrows and sufferings are dire misfortunes, something that we would gladly avoid. By way of a test, let us not take this attitude but assume that for a certain reason we ourselves brought about these sorrows, sufferings, and obstacles, realizing that owing to our earlier lives—if there have actually been such lives—we have become in a sense more imperfect because of what we have done. After all, we do not only become more perfect through the successive incarnations but also, in a certain respect, more imperfect. When we have affronted or injured some human being, are we not more imperfect than we were before? We have not only affronted that person, we have taken something away from ourselves; as a personality taken as a whole, our worth would be greater if we had not done this thing. Many such actions are marked on our score and our imperfection remains because of them. If we have affronted some human being and desire to regain our previous worth, what must happen? We must make compensation for the affront, we must place into the world a counterbalancing deed, we must discover some means of compelling ourselves to overcome something. And if we think in this way about our sufferings and sorrows, we shall be able in many instances to say: These sufferings and sorrows, if we surmount them, give us strength to overcome our imperfections. Through suffering we can make progress.

In normal life we do not think in this way; we set our face against suffering. But we can also say the following: Every sorrow, every suffering, every obstacle in life should be an indication of the fact that we have within us a person who is cleverer than we ourselves are. Although the person we ourselves are is the one of whom we are conscious, we regard this person for a time as being the less clever; within us we have a cleverer person who slumbers in the depths of our soul. With our ordinary consciousness we resist sorrows and sufferings but the cleverer person leads us toward these sufferings in defiance of our consciousness because by overcoming them we can strip off something. The cleverer person guides us to the sorrows and sufferings, directs us to undergo them. To begin with, this may be an oppressive thought but it carries with it no obligation; we can use it, if we so wish, once only by way of trial. We can say: Within us there is a cleverer person who guides us to sufferings and sorrows, to something that in our conscious life we should like most of all to have avoided. We think of this aspect of ourselves as the cleverer person. In this way we are led to the realization that many find disturbing, namely that this cleverer person guides us always toward what we do not like. This, then, we will take as an assumption: There is a cleverer person within us who guides us to what we do not like in order that we may make progress.

But let us still do something else. Let us take our joys, our advantages, our happinesses, and say to ourselves, again by way of trial: How would it be if you were to conceive the idea—irrespectively of how it tallies with the actual reality—

that you have simply not deserved these happinesses, these advantages; they have come to you through the grace of higher, spiritual powers. It need not be so in every case, but we will assume, by way of a test, that all our sorrows and sufferings were brought about because the cleverer person within us guided us to them, because we recognize that in consequence of our imperfections they were necessary for us and that we can overcome them only through such experiences. And then we assume the opposite: That our happinesses are not due to our own merit but have been bestowed upon us by spiritual powers.

Again this thought may be a bitter pill for the vain to swallow, but if, as a test, we are capable of forming such a thought with all intensity, we will be led to the feeling—because again it undergoes a transformation and insofar as it lacks effectiveness, rectifies itself: In you there lives something that has nothing to do with your ordinary consciousness, that lies deeper than anything you have experienced consciously in this life; there is a cleverer person within you who gladly turns to the eternal, divine-spiritual powers pervading the world. Then it becomes an inner certainty that behind the outer there is an inner, higher individuality. Through such thought exercises we grow to be conscious of the eternal, spiritual core of our being, and this is of extraordinary importance. So there again we have something which it lies in our power to carry out.

In every respect anthroposophy can be a guide, not only toward knowledge of the existence of another world, but toward feeling oneself as a citizen of another world, as an individuality who passes through many incarnations.

There are experiences of still a third kind. Admittedly it will be more difficult to make use of these experiences for the purpose of gaining an inner knowledge of karma and reincarnation. But even if what will now be said is difficult, it can again be used by way of trial. And if it is honestly applied to external life it will dawn upon us clearly—as a probability to begin with, but then as an ever-growing certainty—that our present life is connected with an earlier one.

Let us assume that in our present life between birth and death we have already reached or passed our thirtieth year. (Those below that age may also have corresponding experiences.) We reflect about the fact that somewhere near our thirtieth year we were brought into contact with some person in the outside world, that between the ages of thirty and forty many different connections have been established with human beings in the outside world. These connections seem to have been made during the most mature stage of our life so that our whole being was involved in them. Reflection discloses that it is indeed so. But reflection based on the principles and knowledge of spiritual science can lead us to realize the truth of what will now be said—not as the outcome of mere reflection but of spiritual-scientific investigation. What I am saying has not been discovered merely through logical thinking: it has been established by spiritual-scientific research, but logical thinking can confirm the facts and find them reasonable. We know how the several members of the human constitution unfold in the course of life: in the seventh year, the ether body; in the fourteenth year, the astral body; in the twenty-first year the sentient soul, in the twenty-eighth year the intellectual or mind soul, and in the thirty-fifth year the consciousness soul (spiritual soul). Reflecting on this, we can say: In the period from the thirtieth year to the fortieth year we are concerned with the unfolding of the mind soul and the spiritual soul.

The mind soul and the spiritual soul are those forces in our nature that bring us into the closest contact of all with the outer physical world, for they unfold at the very age in life when our intercourse with that world is more active than at any other time. In earliest childhood, the forces belonging to our physical body are directed, determined, activated, by what is still entirely enclosed within us. The causal element engendered in previous incarnations, whatever went with us through the gate of death, the spiritual forces we have garnered—everything we bring with us from the earlier life works and weaves in the upbuilding of our physical body. It is at work unceasingly and invisibly from within outward; as the years go by, this influence diminishes and the period of life approaches when the old forces have produced the body and we confront the world with a finished organism: what we bear within us has come to expression in our external body. At about the thirtieth year—it may be somewhat earlier or somewhat later—we confront the world in the most strongly physical sense; in our intercourse with the world we are connected more closely with the physical plane than during any other period of life. We may think that the relationships in life into which we now enter are more physically intelligible than any others, but the fact is that such relationships are least of all connected with the forces that work and weave in us from birth onward. Nevertheless we may take it for granted that at about the age of thirty we are not led by chance to people who are destined, precisely then, to appear in our environment. We must far rather assume that there too our karma is at work, that these people too have something to do with one of our earlier incarnations.

Facts of spiritual science investigated at various times show that very often the people with whom we come into contact somewhere around our thirtieth year are related to us in such a way that in most cases we were connected with them at the beginning of the immediately preceding incarnation—or it may have been earlier still—as parents, or brothers or sisters. At first this seems a strange and astonishing fact. Although it need not inevitably be so, many cases indicate to spiritual-scientific investigation that in very truth our parents, or those who were by our side at the beginning of our previous life, who gave us our place in the physical world but from whom in later life we grew away, are karmically connected with us in such a way that in our new life we are not again guided to them in early childhood but only when we have come most completely onto the physical plane. It need not always be exactly like this, for spiritual-scientific research shows very frequently that it is not until a subsequent incarnation that those who are then our parents, brothers or sisters, or blood relations in general, are the people we found around us in the present incarnation at about the time of our thirtieth year. So the acquaintances we make somewhere about the age of thirty in any one incarnation may have been, or will be, persons related to us by blood in a previous or subsequent incarnation. It is therefore useful to say to oneself: The personalities with whom life brings you in contact in your thirties were once around you as parents or brothers and sisters or you can anticipate that in one of your next incarnations they will have this relationship with you.

The reverse also holds good. If we think of those personalities whom we choose least of all voluntarily through forces suitable for application on the physical plane—that is to say, our parents, our brothers and sisters who were around us at the beginning of life—if we think of these personalities we shall very often find that precisely those who accompany us into life from childhood onward were deliberately chosen by us in another incarnation to be near us while we were in the thirties. In other words, in the middle of the preceding life we ourselves chose out those who in the present life have become our parents, brothers or sisters.

So the remarkable and very interesting fact emerges that our relationships with the personalities with whom we come to be associated are not the same in the successive incarnations; also that we do not encounter these people at the same age in life as previously. Neither can it be said that exactly the opposite holds good. Furthermore it is not the personalities who were with us at the end of an earlier life who are connected, in a different incarnation, with the beginning of our life, but those with whom we were associated in the middle period of life. So neither those personalities with whom we are together at the beginning of life, nor those with us at its end, but those with whom we come into contact in the middle of life, were around us as blood relations at the beginning of an earlier incarnation. Those who were around us then, when our life was beginning, appear in the middle of our present life; and of those who were around us at the beginning of our present life we can anticipate that we shall find ourselves together with them in the middle of one of our subsequent incarnations, that they will then come into connection with us as freely chosen companions in life. Karmic relationships are indeed mysterious.

What I have now said is the outcome of spiritual-scientific investigation. But I repeat: In the way opened up by this investigation, if we reflect about the inner connections between the beginning of life in one of our incarnations and the middle of life in another, we shall realize that this is not void of sense or usefulness. The other aspect is that when such things are brought to our notice and we adopt an intelligent attitude to them, they bring clarity and illumination. Life is clarified if we do not simply accept such things passively—not to say dull wittedly; it is clarified if we try to grasp, to understand, what comes to us in life in such a way that the relationships that are bound to remain elusive as long as karma is only spoken of in the abstract, become concretely perceptible.

It is useful to reflect about the question: Why is it that in the middle of our life we are actually driven by karma, seemingly with complete mental awareness, to form some acquaintance-ship that does not appear to have been made quite independently and objectively? The reason is that such persons were related to us by blood in the earlier life and our karma leads them to us now because we have some connection with them.

Whenever we reflect in this way about the course of our own life, we shall see that light is shed upon it. Although we may be mistaken in some particular instance, and even if we err in our conclusions ten times over, nevertheless we may well hit upon the truth in regard to someone who comes into our ken. And when such reflections lead us to say: Somewhere or other I have met this person—this thought is like a signpost pointing the way to other things which in different circumstances would not have occurred to us and which, taken in their whole setting, give us ever-growing certainty of the correctness of particular facts.

Karmic connections are not of such a nature that they can be discerned in one sudden flash. The highest, most important facts of knowledge regarding life, those that really do shed light upon it, must be acquired slowly and by degrees. This is not a welcome thought. It is easier to believe that some flash of illumination might enable it to be said: "In an earlier life I was associated with this or that person," or "I myself was this or that individual." It may be tiresome to think that all this must be a matter of knowledge slowly acquired, but that is the case nevertheless. Even if we merely cherish the belief that it might possibly be so, investigation must be repeated time and time again before the belief will become certainty. Even in cases where probability grows constantly stronger, investigation leads us farther. We erect barricades against the spiritual world if we allow ourselves to form instantaneous judgments in these matters.

Try to ponder over what has been said today about the acquaintanceships made in the middle period of life and their connection with individuals who were near to us in a preceding incarnation. This will lead to very fruitful thoughts, especially if taken together with what is said in the book, *The Education of the Child in the Light of Anthroposophy.* It will then be unambiguously clear that the outcome of your reflection tallies with what is set forth in that book.

But an earnest warning must be added to what has been said today. Genuine investigators guard against drawing conclusions; things are allowed to come of themselves. Once the things are there, they are first put to the test of ordinary logic. Repetition will then be impossible of something that recently happened to me, not for the first time, and is very characteristic of the attitude adopted to anthroposophy today. A very clever man—I say this without irony, fully recognizing that he has a brilliant mind—said the following to me: "When I read what is contained in your book, *An Outline of Occult Science*, I am bound to admit that it seems so logical, to tally so completely with other manifest facts in the world, that I cannot help coming to the conclusion that these things could also be discovered through pure reflection; they need not necessarily be the outcome of supersensible investigation. The things said in this book are in no way questionable or dubious; they tally with the reality." I was able to assure this gentleman of my conviction that it would not have been possible for me to discover them through mere reflection, nor that with great respect for his cleverness, could I believe he would have discovered them by that means alone. It is absolutely true that whatever in the domain of spiritual science is capable of being logically comprehended simply cannot be discovered by mere reflection. The fact that some matter can be put to the test of logic and then grasped, should be no ground for doubting its spiritual-scientific origin. On the contrary, I am sure it must be reassuring to know that the communications made by spiritual science can be recognized through logical reflection as being unquestionably correct; it cannot possibly be the ambition of a spiritual investigator to make illogical statements for the sake of inspiring belief! As you see, spiritual investigators themselves cannot take the standpoint that they discover such things through reflection. But if we reflect about things that have been discovered by the methods of spiritual science, they may seem quite logical, even too logical to allow us to believe any longer that they actually come from spiritual-scientific sources. And this applies to everything said to have been the outcome of genuine spiritual-scientific investigation.

If the things that have been said today seem grotesque to begin with, try for one to apply logical thinking to them. Truly, if spiritual facts had not led me to these things, I should not have deduced them from ordinary, logical thinking; but once they have been discovered they can be put to the test of logic. And then it will be found that the more meticulously and conscientiously we set about testing them, the more clearly it will emerge that everything tallies. Even in the case of matters where accuracy cannot really be tested, from the very way in which the various factors fit into their settings, it will be found that they give the impression of being not only in the highest degree probable, but bordering on certainty—as in the case, for example, of what has been said about parents and brothers and sisters in one life and acquaintances made in the middle of another life. Moreover such certainty proves to be well founded when things are put to the test of life itself. In many cases we shall view our own behavior and that of others in a quite different light if we confront someone we meet in the middle period of life as if, in the preceding life, the relationship between us had been that of parent, brother, or sister. The whole relationship will thereby become much more fruitful than if we go through life with drowsy inattentiveness.

And so we can say: More and more, anthroposophy becomes something that does not merely give us knowledge of life but directives as to how to conceive of life's relationships in such a way that light will be shed upon them not only for our own satisfaction, but also for our conduct and tasks in life. It is important to discard the thought that in this way we impair a spontaneous response to life. Only the timid, those who lack a really earnest purpose in life, can believe such a thing. We, however, must realize that by gaining closer knowledge of life we make it more fruitful, inwardly richer. What comes to us in life should be carried, through anthroposophy, into horizons where all our forces become more fertile, more full of confidence, a greater stimulus to hope, than they were before.

Stuttgart, February 21, 1912

*T*he lecture yesterday dealt with questions of karma, and the endeavor was made to speak of them in such a way that they appear to us to be linked with inner processes in the soul, with something that is within our reach. It was said that certain tentative measures can be taken and that in this way a conviction of the truth of the law of karma may be awakened. If such questions are introduced again and again into our studies, this is because it is necessary to realize with increasing clarity how anthroposophy, in the genuine sense of the word, is related to life itself and to the whole of human evolution.

There is no doubt that at least an approximately adequate idea can be formed of the change that will gradually and inevitably take place in all human life if a considerable number of people are convinced of the truths upon which studies such as those of yesterday are based. By steeping themselves in such truths, people's attitude to life will be quite different and life itself will change in consequence.

This brings us to the very important question—and it is a question of conscience for those who enter the anthroposophical movement: What is it, in reality, that makes a person of the modern age into an anthroposophist? Misunderstanding may really arise when endeavors are made to answer this question, for even today many people—including those who belong to us—still confuse the anthroposophical movement with some form of external organization. There is nothing to be said against an external organization, which from a certain point of view must exist in order to make it possible for anthroposophy to be cultivated on the physical plane; but it is important to realize that all human beings whose interest in questions of the spiritual life is earnest and sincere and who wish to deepen their world-view in accordance with the principles of this spiritual movement, can belong to such an organization. From this it is obvious that no dogmatic, positive declaration of belief can be demanded from those who attach themselves to such an organization. But it is a different matter to speak quite precisely of what makes someone of the present age into an anthroposophist.

The conviction that a spiritual world must be taken into account is, of course, the starting point of anthroposophical conviction, and this must always be stressed when anthroposophy is introduced to the public and reference made to its tasks, aims, and present mission in life. But in anthroposophical circles themselves it must be realized that what makes the anthroposophist is something much more definite, much more decisive than the mere conviction of the existence of a spiritual world. After all, this conviction has always been held in circles that were not utterly materialistic. What constitutes a modern anthroposophist and, fundamentally speaking, was not contained in the theosophy of Jacob Boehme, for example, or of other earlier theosophists, is something toward which the efforts of our Western culture are strenuously directed—so much so, on the one side, that such efforts have become characteristic of the strivings of many human beings. But on the other side there is the fact that what particularly characterizes the anthroposophist is still vehemently attacked by external culture and education, is still regarded as nonsense.

We do, of course, learn many things through anthroposophy. We learn about the evolution of humanity, even about the evolution of our earth and planetary system. All these things belong to the fundamentals required by one who desires to become an anthroposophist. But what is of particular importance for the modern anthroposophist is the gaining of conviction with regard to reincarnation and karma. The way in which people gain this conviction, how they succeed in spreading the thought of reincarnation and karma—it is this that from now onward will essentially transform modern life, will create new forms of life, an entirely new social life, of the kind that is necessary if human culture is not to decline but rise to a higher level. Experiences in the life of soul such as were described yesterday are, fundamentally speaking, within the reach of every modern person, and if only we have sufficient energy and tenacity of purpose we will certainly become inwardly convinced of the truth of reincarnation and karma. But the whole character of our present age is pitted against what must be the aim of true anthroposophy.

Perhaps this fundamental character of our present age nowhere expresses itself so radically and typically as in the fact that considerable interest is shown in the central questions of religion, in the evolution of the world and of the human being, and even in karma and reincarnation. When such questions extend to the specific tenets of religions—concerning, let us say, the nature of the Buddha or of Christ—when such questions are discussed today, evidence of widespread interest will be apparent. But this interest fades the moment we speak in concrete detail about how anthroposophy must penetrate into every domain of external life. That interest dwindles is, after all, very understandable. People have their places in external life, they hold various positions in the world. With all its organizations and institutions the modern world appears not unlike a vast emporium with the individual human being working in it as a wheel, or something of the kind. This indeed is what we feel ourselves to be, with our labor, our anxieties, our occupation from morning till evening, and we know nothing beyond the fact that we are obliged to fit into this outer world order. Side by side with these conditions, then, arises the question that must exercise every soul who is able to look even a little beyond what everyday life offers: it is the question of the soul's destiny, of the beginning and end of the soul's life, its connection with divine-spiritual beings and powers holding sway in the universe. And between what everyday life with its cares and anxieties brings to human beings and what we receive in the domain of anthroposophy yawns a deep abyss.

It may be said that for most people of the present age there is almost no harmony between their convictions and what they do and think in their outer, everyday life. If some concrete question is raised in public and dealt with in the light of spiritual science or anthroposophy, it will at once be evident that the interest which was still there in the case of general questions of religion and the like, no longer exists when it comes to matters of a really concrete kind. It cannot, of course, be expected that anthroposophy will at once make its way into life, that everyone will immediately bring it to expression in whatever they are doing. But the world must be made to realize that it is the mission of spiritual science to introduce into life, to incorporate in life, everything that will emanate from a soul who has become convinced of the truth of the ideas of reincarnation and karma. And so the characteristic stamp of modern anthroposophists may be said to be that they are on the way to acquiring a firmly based, inner conviction of the validity of the idea of reincarnation and karma. All the rest will then follow of itself.

Naturally it will not do to think: Now, reinforced with the knowledge of reincarnation and karma, I shall at once be able to grapple with external life. That, of course, is not possible.

The essential thing is to understand how the truths of reincarnation and karma can penetrate into external life in such a way that they become its guiding principles.

Now let us consider how karma works through the different incarnations. When human beings come into the world, their powers and capacities must, after all, be regarded as the effects of causes they themselves engendered in earlier incarnations. If this idea is led to its consistent conclusion, all human beings must be treated as if they were a kind of enigma, as beings hovering in the dark foundations of their earlier incarnations. If this idea of karma is put earnestly into effect a significant change will be brought about, not in methods of education only but in the whole of life. If that were achieved, the idea of karma, instead of being merely an anthroposophical idea, would be transformed into something that takes hold of practical life itself, would become a really potent factor in life.

But all external life as it presents itself today is the picture of a social condition which, in its development, has excluded, has indeed refuted, the idea of reincarnation and karma. External life today is organized almost as if there were a deliberate desire to quash any possibility of people being able, through their own inner development, to discover the reality of reincarnation and karma. In point of fact there is, for example, nothing more hostile to a real conviction of reincarnation and karma than the principle that people must be remunerated, must receive wages corresponding to their actual labor. To speak like this seems utterly eccentric! Do not, however, take this example to imply that anthroposophy would wish to throw to the winds the principles of an established practice and to introduce a new social order overnight! That cannot be. But people must become alive to the thought that no fundamental conviction of reincarnation can ever flourish in a world order in which it is held that there must be a direct correspondence between wages and labor, in which people are obliged, through the labor they perform, to obtain the necessities of life. Naturally the prevailing conditions must remain, to begin with, for it will be clear, above all to anthroposophists, that what exists is in turn the outcome of karmic law and in this sense is justified and inevitable. But it is absolutely essential for people to be able to realize that what can, and must, ensue from recognition of the idea of reincarnation and karma, unfolds as a new seed in the organism of our world order.

Above all it follows from the idea of karma that we should not feel ourselves to have been placed by chance into the world order, into the positions in which we find ourselves in life; on the contrary, we should feel that a kind of subconscious decision of the will underlies it, that as the result of our earlier incarnations, before we passed into this earthly existence out of the spiritual world between death and a new birth, we resolved in the spiritual world—a resolve we merely forgot when we incarnated in the body—to occupy the very position in which we now find ourselves. Consequently it is the outcome of a prenatal, preearthly decision of the will that we are assigned to our particular place in life and have the actual inclination to steer toward the blows of destiny that befall us. If we then become convinced of the truth of the law of karma, we will inevitably begin to incline toward, even possibly to love, the position in the world in which we have placed ourselves—no matter what it may be.

You may say: You are telling us very strange things. They may be all very well for poets or writers, or others engaged in spiritual pursuits. To such people you do well to preach that they should love, delight in, be devoted to, their particular positions in life. But what of all those human beings whose situations, in their very nature and with the labors they involve, cannot possibly be particularly welcome but will inevitably evoke the feeling of belonging to the neglected or oppressed? Who would deny that a large proportion of the efforts made in modern civilization aim at introducing into life continuous improvements which may help to get rid of the discontent at having been placed in such unpleasant situations? How numerous are the different institutions and sectarian endeavors to better life in all directions in order that even from the external aspect the earthly life of humanity might be bearable!

None of these endeavors reckons with the fact that the kind of discontent inevitably brought by life to numbers of people today is connected in many respects with the whole course taken by the evolution of humanity; that fundamentally speaking, the way in which people developed in past ages led to karma of this kind, and that out of the combined working of these different karmas the present state of human civilization has proceeded. In characterizing this state of civilization we can only say that it is complex in the highest degree. It must also be said that the connection between what people do, what they carry out, and what they love, is weakening all the time. And if we were to count those people who in their positions in external life today are obliged to engage in some activity that goes much against the grain, their number would by far exceed the number of those who affirm: I can only say that I love my external occupation, that it brings me happiness and contentment.

Only recently I heard of a strange statement made by someone to a friend. He said: "When I look back over my life in all its details I confess that if I had to live through it again from childhood to the present moment, I should do exactly the same things I have done up to now." The friend replied: "Then you are one of those most rarely to be found at the present time!" The friend was probably right, as far as most people of the modern age are concerned. Not many of our contemporaries would assert that, if it depended on them, they would without hesitation begin life all over again, together with everything it has brought in the way of happiness, sorrow, blows of fate, obstacles, and would be quite content if everything were exactly the same again.

It cannot be said that the fact just mentioned—namely that there are so few people nowadays who would be willing to recapitulate the karma of their present life together with all its details—it cannot be said that this is unconnected with what the prevailing cultural state of humanity has brought in its train. Our life has become more complex but it has been made so by the different karmas of the personalities living on the earth today. Of that there can be no doubt at all. Nor will those who have the slightest insight into the course taken by human evolution be able to speak of any possibility of a less complicated life in the future. On the contrary, the complexity of external life will steadily increase and however many activities are taken over from human beings in the future by machines, there can be very few lives of happiness in this present incarnation unless conditions quite different from those now prevailing are brought about. And these different conditions must be the result of the human soul being convinced of the truth of reincarnation and karma.

From this it will be realized that something quite different must run parallel with the complexity of external civilization. What is it that will be necessary to ensure that people become more and more deeply permeated with the truth of reincarnation and karma? What will be necessary in order that the concept of reincarnation and karma may comparatively soon instill itself into our education, take hold of human beings even in childhood, in the way that children now are convinced of the truth of the Copernican theory of the universe?

What was it that enabled the Copernican theory of the universe to lay hold of people's minds? This Copernican world system has had a peculiar destiny. I am not going to speak about the theory itself but only about its entry into the world. Remember that this world system was thought out by a Christian dignitary and that Copernicus's own conception of it was such that he felt it permissible to dedicate to the Pope the work in which he elaborated his hypothesis. He believed that his conclusions were entirely in keeping with Christianity.[1] Was any proof of the truth of Copernicanism available at that time? Could anyone have demonstrated the truth of its conclusions? Nobody could have done so. Yet think of the rapidity with which it made its way into humanity. Since when has proof been available? To the extent to which it is correct, only since the fifties of the nineteenth century, only since Foucault's experiment with the pendulum.[2] Before then there was no proof that the earth rotates. It is nonsense to state that Copernicus was also able to prove what he had presented and investigated as a hypothesis; this also holds good of the statement that the earth rotates on its axis.

Only since it was discovered that a swinging pendulum has the tendency to maintain the plane of its oscillation even in opposition to the rotation of the earth and that if a long pendulum is allowed to swing, then the direction of oscillation rotates in relation to the earth's surface, could the conclusion be drawn: It is the earth beneath the pendulum that must have

1. Nicholas Copernicus (1473-1543) became a Church dignitary in Frauenburg. His celebrated astronomical work, *De revolutionibus orbium coelestium*, had been dedicated to Pope Paul III, but was not printed until 1543, in Nurnberg. Although protected, to begin with, by the dedication to the Pope, in 1615 it was put on the Index of books forbidden to Catholics, remaining there until 1822, when the ban was officially lifted by the Vatican on works dealing with the earth's motion and the fixed position of the sun.

2. In 1851, at the Pantheon in Paris, Leon Foucault demonstrated the diurnal motion of the earth by the rotation of the plane of oscillation of a freely suspended, long and heavy pendulum, and again the following year by means of his invention of the gyroscope.

rotated. This experiment, which afforded the first actual proof that the earth moves, was not made until the nineteenth century. Earlier than that there was no wholly satisfactory possibility of regarding Copernicanism as being anything more than a hypothesis. Nevertheless its effect upon the human mind in the modern age was so great that until the year 1822 his book was on the Index, in spite of the fact that Copernicus had believed it permissible to dedicate it to the Pope. Not until the year 1822 was the book on which Copernicanism was based removed from the Index—before, therefore, any real proof of its correctness was available. The power of the impulse with which the Copernican theory of the universe instilled itself into the human mind finally compelled the Church to recognize it as non-heretical.

I have always considered it deeply symptomatic that this knowledge of the earth's motion was first imparted to me as a boy at school, not by an ordinary teacher, but by a priest.[3] Who can possibly doubt that Copernicanism has taken firm root, even in the minds of children? I am not speaking now of its truths and its errors. If culture is not to fall into decline, the truths of reincarnation and karma must take equally firm root— but the time that humanity has at its disposal for this is not as long as it was in the case of Copernicanism. And it is incumbent upon those who call themselves anthroposophists today to play their part in ensuring that the truths of reincarnation and karma shall flow even into the minds of the young. This of course does not mean that anthroposophists who have children should inculcate this into them as a dogma. Insight is what is needed.

---

3. This was Franz Maraz, the priest at Neudorff, near Wiener Neustadt. Maraz was a Hungarian, later Canon at Oedenburg, and held high offices. In his autobiography, *The Course of My Life*, Rudolf Steiner says of him: "The image of this man was deeply engraved in my soul and throughout my life he has come again and again into my memory."

I have not spoken of Copernicanism without reason. From the success of Copernicanism we can learn what will ensure the spread of the ideas of reincarnation and karma. What, then, were the factors responsible for the rapid spread of Copernicanism? I shall now be saying something terribly heretical, something that will seem quite atrocious to the modern mind. But what matters is that anthroposophy shall be taken as earnestly and as profoundly as Christianity was taken by the first Christians, who also arrayed themselves against the conditions then prevailing. If anthroposophy is not taken with equal seriousness by those who profess to be its adherents, it cannot achieve for humanity what must be achieved.

I have now to say something quite atrocious, and it is this: Copernicanism, what we learn today as the Copernican theory of the universe—the great merits of which and therewith its significance as a cultural factor of the very first order are truly not disputed—this theory was able to take root in the human soul because to be a believer in this world system it is possible to be a superficial thinker. Superficiality and externality contribute to a more rapid conviction of Copernicanism. This is not to minimize its significance for humanity. But it can truly be said that people need not be very profound, need not deepen themselves inwardly, before accepting Copernicanism; they must far rather externalize their thinking. And indeed a high degree of externalization has been responsible for trivial utterances such as those to be found in modern monistic books, where it is said, actually with a touch of fervor: Compared with other worlds, the earth, as humanity's habitation, is a speck of dust in the universe.[4] This is a futile statement for the simple reason that this "speck of dust," with all that belongs to it, is a vital concern of human beings in terrestrial existence,

---

4. cp. Herbert Spencer (1820–1903).

and the other worlds in the universe with which the earth is compared are of less importance to us. The evolution of humanity was obliged to become completely externalized to be quickly capable of accepting Copernicanism.

But what must people do in order to assimilate the teaching of reincarnation and karma? This teaching must meet with far more rapid success if humanity is not to fall into decline. What is it that is necessary to enable it to take footing, even in the minds of children? Externalization was necessary for the acceptance of Copernicanism; inner deepening is necessary for realizing the truths of reincarnation and karma, the capacity to take in earnest such things as were spoken of yesterday, to penetrate into intimate matters of the life of soul, into things that every soul must experience in the deep foundations of its own core of being. The results and consequences of Copernicanism in present-day culture are paraded everywhere nowadays, in every popular publication, and the fact that all these things can be presented in pictures—even, whenever possible, in films—is regarded as a very special triumph. This already characterizes the tremendous externalization of our cultural life.

Little can be shown in pictures, little can be actually communicated about the intimacies of the truths embraced in the words "reincarnation" and "karma." To realize that the conviction of reincarnation and karma is well founded depends upon a deepened understanding of such things as were said in the lecture yesterday. And so the very opposite of what is habitual in the external culture of today is necessary if the idea of reincarnation and karma is to take root in humanity. That is why such insistence is laid upon this deepening—in the domain of anthroposophy too. Although it cannot be denied that certain schematic presentations may be useful for an intellectual grasp of fundamental truths, it must nevertheless be realized that what is of primary importance in anthroposophy is to turn our attention to the laws operating in the depths of the soul, to what is at work inwardly, beneath the forces of the soul, as the outer, physical laws are at work in the worlds of time and space.

There is very little understanding today of the laws of karma. Is there anyone who as an enlightened person in the sense of modern culture, would not maintain that humanity has outgrown the stage of childhood, the stage of faith, and has reached the stage of adulthood where knowledge can take the place of faith? Such utterances are to be heard perpetually and give rise to a great deal that deludes people in the outside world but should never delude anthroposophists—utterances to the effect that faith must be replaced by knowledge.

But none of these tirades on the subject of faith and knowledge take into consideration what may be called karmic relationships in life. One who is capable of spiritual-scientific investigation and observes particularly pious, devotional natures among people of the present time, will ask: Why is this or that person so pious, so devout? Why is there in these people the fervor of faith, the enthusiasm, a veritable genius for religious devoutness, for directing their thoughts to the supersensible world? If the investigator asks these questions he or she will find a remarkable answer to them. If in the case of these devout people in whom faith did not, perhaps, become an important factor in their lives until a comparatively advanced age, we go back to earlier incarnations, the strange fact is discovered that in preceding incarnations, these individualities were people of learning, people of knowledge. The scholarship, the element of intelligence in their earlier incarnations has been transformed, in the present incarnation, into the element of faith. There we have one of those strange facts of karma.

Forgive me if I now say something that nobody sitting here will take amiss but would shock many in the outside world who swear by and are willing to accept only what is presented by the senses and the intellect that is dependent on the brain. In people who because of strongly materialistic tendencies no longer desire to have faith, but knowledge only, we find—and this is a very enigmatic fact—dull-wittedness, obtuseness, in the preceding incarnation. Genuine investigation of the different incarnations, therefore, yields this strange result, that ardently devout natures, people who are not fanatic but inwardly steadfast in their devotion to the higher worlds, developed the quality of faith they now possess on the foundation of knowledge gained in earlier incarnations; whereas knowledge founded on materialism is the outcome of obtuseness to views of the world in earlier incarnations.

Think how the whole conception of life changes if the gaze is widened from the immediate present to what the human individuality experiences through the different incarnations!

Many a quality upon which people pride themselves in the present incarnation assumes a strange aspect when considered in the setting of how it was acquired in the preceding incarnation. Viewed in the light of reincarnation, many things will seem less incredible. We need think only of how, with these inner forces of soul, a person develops in one incarnation; we need observe only the power of faith in the soul, the power of soul that may inhere in faith and belief in something that as supersensible reality transcends the phenomena of ordinary sense perception. A materialistic monist may strongly oppose this, insisting that knowledge alone is valid, that faith has no sure foundation—but against this there is another fact, namely that the power of faith in the soul has a life-giving effect upon the astral body, whereas absence of faith, skepticism, parches and dries it up. Faith works upon the astral body as nourishment works upon the physical body. And is it not important to realize what faith does for human beings, for their well-being, for their healthiness of soul, and—because this is also the determining factor for physical health—for their body too? Is it not strange that on the one side there should be the desire to abolish faith, while on the other side someone who is incapable of faith is bound to have a barren, withered astral body? Even by observing the one life only this can be recognized. It is not necessary to survey a series of incarnations, for it can be recognized in the one. We can therefore say: Lack of faith, skepticism, dries up our astral body; if we lack faith we impoverish ourselves and in the following incarnation our individuality is drained dry. Lack of faith makes us obtuse in the next incarnation, incapable of acquiring knowledge. To contrast knowledge with faith is the outcome of worldly, jejune logic. For those who have insight into these things, all the palaver about faith and knowledge has about as much sense as there would be in a discussion where one speaker declares that up to now human progress has depended more upon men, while the other maintains that women have played the more important part. In the stage of childhood, therefore, the one sex is held to be more important, but at the present stage, the other! For those who are cognizant of the spiritual facts it is clear that faith and knowledge are related to each other as the two sexes are related in outer, physical life. This must be borne in mind as a trenchant and significant fact—and then we shall be able to see the matter in its true light. The parallelism goes so far that it may be said: Just as the sex usually alternates in the successive incarnations, so, as a rule, an incarnation with a more intellectual trend follows one more inclined toward faith, then again toward intellectuality, and so forth. There are, of course, exceptions—there may be several consecutive male or female incarnations. But as a rule these qualities are mutually fruitful and complementary.

Other qualities in the human being are also complementary in a similar way, for example, the two qualities of soul we will call the capacity for love and inner strength.

Self-reliance, harmonious inner life, a feeling of our own sure foundations, the inner assurance that we know what we have to do in life—in this connection too the working of karma alternates in the different incarnations. The outstanding stamp of the one personality is loving devotion to its own environment, forgetfulness of self, surrender to what is around it. Such an incarnation will alternate with one in which the individual feels the urge not to lose itself in the outer world but to strengthen itself inwardly, applying this strength to bring about its own progress. This latter urge must not, of course, degenerate into lack of love, any more than the former urge must not degenerate, as it might well do, into a complete loss of one's own self. These two tendencies again belong together. And it must be constantly emphasized that when anthroposophists have the desire to sacrifice themselves, such desire is not enough. Many people would like to sacrifice themselves all the time—they feel happy in so doing—but before anyone can make a sacrifice of real value to the world they must have the strength required for it. Individuals must first be something before they can usefully sacrifice themselves; otherwise the sacrifice of egohood is not of much value. Moreover in a certain respect a kind of egoism—although it is repressed—a kind of laziness, is present when people make no effort to develop, to persevere in their strivings, so that what they can achieve is of real value.

It might seem—but please do not misunderstand this—as though we were preaching lovelessness. The outer world is very prone today to reproach anthroposophists by saying: You aim at perfecting your own souls, you strive for the progress of your own souls. You become egoists! It must be admitted that many capricious fancies, many failings and errors may arise in people's endeavors toward perfection. What very often appears to be the principle of development adopted among anthroposophists does not by any means always call for admiration. Behind this striving there is often a great deal of hidden egoism.

On the other side it must be emphasized that we are living in an epoch of civilization when devoted willingness for sacrifice only too often goes to waste. Although lack of love is in evidence everywhere, there is also an enormous waste of love and willingness for sacrifice. This must not be misunderstood; but it should be realized that love, if it is not accompanied by wisdom in the conduct of life, by wise insight into the existing conditions, can be very misplaced and therefore harmful rather than beneficial. We are living in the age when it is necessary for something that can help the soul to progress—again something that anthroposophy can bring—to penetrate into the souls of a large number of human beings, inwardly enriching and fertilizing them. For the sake of the next incarnation and also for the sake of their activity between death and a new birth, people must be capable of performing deeds that are not based merely upon old customs, but are in essence new. These things must be regarded with great earnestness for it must be established that anthroposophy has a mission, that it is like a seed of culture that must grow and come to flower in the future. But it can best be seen how this is fulfilled in life if we bear in mind karmic connections such as those between faith and reason, love and self-reliance.

A person who in accordance with the view prevailing nowadays is convinced that after having passed through the gate of death the only prospect is that of an extraterrestrial eternity somewhere beyond this world, will never be able truly to assess the soul's progress, for that person will say: If indeed there is such a thing as progress you cannot achieve it, for your

existence is only transitory, you are in this world for a short
time only and all you can do is to prepare for that other world.

It is a fact that our greatest wisdom in life comes from our
failures: we learn from our failures, gather the most wisdom
from the very things where we have not been successful. Ask
yourselves seriously how often you have the opportunity of
repeating a mistake, in exactly the same circumstances as
before—you will find that such a situation rarely occurs. And
would not life be utterly without purpose if the wisdom we can
acquire from our mistakes were to be lost to earthly humanity?
Only if we can come back again, if in a new life we can put into
effect the experiences gained in earlier lives—only then does
life acquire meaning and purpose. In either case it is senseless to
strive for real progress in this earthly existence if it is regarded
as the only one, and also for an eternity beyond the earth.

And it is particularly senseless for those who think that all
existence comes to an end when they have passed through the
gate of death. What strength, what energy and confidence in
life would be people gain if they knew that they can turn to
account in a new life whatever forces are apparently lost to
them? Modern culture is as it is because so very little was
gathered for it in the previous incarnations of human beings.
Truly, souls have become impoverished in the course of their
incarnations. How is this to be explained?

In long past ages, before the Mystery of Golgotha, people
were endowed with an ancient clairvoyance and magical forces
of will. And it continued to be so on into the Christian era. But
in the final stages of this ancient clairvoyance it was only the
evil forces, the demonic forces, that came down from the
higher worlds. There are many references in the Gospels to
demonic natures around Christ Jesus. Human souls had lost
their original connection with the divine-spiritual forces and
beings. And then Christ came to humankind. Human beings

who are living at the present time have had perhaps two or three incarnations since then, each according to their karma. The influence exercised by Christianity until now could only have been what it is, because human souls were feeble, drained of force. Christianity could not unfold its whole inner power because of the feebleness of human souls. The extent to which this was so can be gauged if a different wave in human civilization is considered—the wave which in the East led to Buddhism. Buddhism has the conviction of the truth of reincarnation and karma but in such a form that it regards the purpose and task of progress in evolution to consist in leading human beings away from life as quickly as possible. In the East a wave was astir in which there was no urge for existence. So we see how everything that should inspire people with determination to fulfill the mission of the earth has fallen away from those who belong to the wave of culture that is the bearer of Buddhism. And if Buddhism were to spread widely in the West, this would be a proof that souls of the feeblest type are very numerous, for it is these souls who would become Buddhists. Wherever Buddhism in some form might appear in the West, this would be a proof that the souls in question want to evade the mission of the earth, to escape from it as quickly as they can, being incapable of tackling it.

When Christianity was spreading in the south of Europe and was being adopted by the peoples of the north, the force of instinct in these northern souls was strong and powerful. They absorbed Christianity, but, to begin with, its external aspects only could be brought into prominence, that is to say, those aspects which render it so important for people today to deepen their experience of the Christ impulse, so that this Christ impulse may become the inmost power of the soul itself and the soul may grow inwardly richer as it lives on toward the future. Human souls have passed through incarnations of weakness, of uncertainty, and, to begin with, Christianity was an external support. But now the epoch has come when souls must become inwardly strong and vigorous. Therefore as time goes on, what the individual does in outer life will be of little consequence. What will be essential is that the soul shall find its own footing, shall deepen itself, acquire insight into how the inner reality can be inculcated into the outer life, how the earth's mission can be permeated through and through with the consciousness, the strong inner realization born from conviction of the truths of reincarnation and karma.

Even if no more than a humble beginning is made in the direction of enabling these truths to penetrate into life, this humble beginning is nevertheless of untold significance. The more we learn to judge people according to their inner faculties, to deepen life inwardly, the more we help to bring about what must be the basic character of a future humanity. External life will become increasingly complicated—that cannot be prevented—but souls will find their way to one another through a deepened inner life. The individual may engage in this or that outer activity—but it is the inner richness of the soul that in the anthroposophical life will unite individual souls and enable them to work to the end that this anthroposophical life shall flow more and more strongly into external culture. We know that the whole of our outer life is strengthened when the soul discovers its reality in anthroposophy; individuals pursuing occupations and vocations of every kind in outer life find themselves united. The soul of external cultural life itself is created through what is given us in anthroposophy: benediction of the external life. To make this benediction possible, consciousness of the great law of karma must first awaken in the soul. The more we advance into the future, the more must the individual soul be able to feel within itself the benediction of the whole of life.

Outer laws and institutions will make life so complicated that people may well lose their bearings altogether. But by realizing the truth of the law of karma the knowledge will be born in the soul of what it must do in order to find, from within, its path through the world. This path will best be found when the things of the world are regulated by the inner life of soul. There are certain things that go on quite satisfactorily because everyone follows the impulse that is an unerring guide. An example is that of walking along the street. People are not yet given precise instructions to step aside to one side of the pavement or the other. Yet two people walking toward each other very rarely collide, because they obey an inner instinct. Otherwise everyone would need to have a policeman at their side ordering them to move to the right or left. Certain circles would really like everyone to have a policeman on one side and a doctor on the other all the time—but that is not yet in the realm of possibility! Nevertheless progress can best be made in those things where a person is guided by an inner, spontaneous impulse. In the social life this must lead to respect for human beings, respect for human dignity. And this can be achieved only if we understand individuals as they can be understood when the law of reincarnation and karma is taken into account. This social life among human beings can be raised to a higher level only when the significance of this law takes root in the soul. This is shown most clearly of all by concrete observation such as that of the connection between ardent faith and knowledge, between love and self-reliance.

These two lectures have not been given without purpose. The real importance does not lie so much in what is actually said—it could be put in a different way. But what is of prime importance is that those who profess to adhere to anthroposophy as a cultural movement shall be so thoroughly steeped in the ideas of reincarnation and karma that they realize how life must inevitably become different if every human soul is conscious of these truths. The cultural life of the modern age has taken shape with the exclusion of consciousness of reincarnation and karma. And the all-important factor that will be introduced through anthroposophy is that these truths will take real hold of life, that they will penetrate culture and in so doing essentially transform it.

Just as a modern person who says that reincarnation and karma are fantastic nonsense, for it can be seen how human beings are born and how they die—something passes out at death but as that cannot be seen there is no need to take account of it—just as someone who speaks in this way is related to one who says: What passes away cannot be seen, but this law can be taken into account and those who do so will for the first time find all life's happenings intelligible, will be able to grasp things that are otherwise inexplicable…so will the culture of today be related to the culture of the future, in which the laws, the teachings of reincarnation and karma will be contained. And although these two laws—as thoughts held by humanity in general—have played no part in the development of present-day culture, they will certainly play a very leading part in all culture of the future.

Anthroposophists must feel and be conscious of the fact that in this way they are helping to bring about the birth of a new culture. This feeling of the enormous significance in life of the ideas of reincarnation and karma can be a bond of union among a group of human beings today, no matter what their external circumstances may be. And those who are eventually held together by such a feeling can find their way to one another only through anthroposophy.

L E C T U R E   F I V E

Berlin, March 5, 1912

*F*or many years past we have been studying anthroposophical truths, details of anthroposophical knowledge, trying to approach them from different sides and to assimilate them. In the course of the lectures now being given, and those yet to come, it will be well to ask ourselves what anthroposophy should and can give to the people of our time. We know a good deal of the content of anthroposophy and we can therefore approach the question with a certain basis of understanding.

We must above all remember that the anthroposophical life, the anthroposophical movement itself, must be clearly distinguished—in our minds at any rate—from any kind of special organization, from anything to which the name "society" might be given. The whole character of modern life will of course make it more and more necessary for those who want to cultivate anthroposophy to unite in a corporate sense; but this is made necessary more by the character of life outside than by the content or attitude of anthroposophy itself. Anthroposophy in itself could be made known to the world in the same way as anything else—as chemistry, for instance— and its truths could be accessible just as in the case of the truths of chemistry or mathematics. How individuals assimilate anthroposophy and make it a real impulse in their lives could then be a matter for individuals themselves. A society or any kind of corporate body for the cultivation of anthroposophy is made necessary because anthroposophy as such comes into our epoch as something new, as entirely new knowledge, which must be received into the spiritual life of humanity. Those who have not entered the sphere of anthroposophical life need a special preparation of their souls and hearts as well as the constitution of soul belonging to the present age. Such preparation can be acquired only through the life and activities in our groups and meetings. There we adapt ourselves to a certain trend of thinking and feeling, so that we realize the significance of matters that people in the outside world who know nothing of anthroposophy will naturally regard as fantastic nonsense. It might, of course, be argued that anthroposophy could also be made more widely known through public lectures given to entirely unprepared listeners; but those who belong to our groups in a more intimate sense will realize that the whole tone, the whole manner of delivering a lecture to an unprepared public must necessarily be different from that of a lecture given to those who through an inner urge and through their whole attitude, are able to take seriously what the general public would not yet be able to accept. Quite certainly this stage of things will not improve in the immediate future—on the contrary, the opposition will become stronger and stronger. Opposition to anthroposophy in every domain will increase in the outside world, just because it is in the highest degree necessary for our age, and because what is the most essential at any particular time always encounters the strongest resistance.

It may be asked: Why is this so? Why do human hearts resist so vehemently just what is most needed in their epoch? An anthroposophist should be able to understand this, but it is too complicated a matter to be made even remotely clear to an unprepared public.

The student of anthroposophy knows of the existence of luciferic forces, of luciferic beings who have lagged behind the general process of evolution. They work through human hearts and souls and it is to their greatest advantage to launch their fiercest attacks at times when, in reality, there is the strongest urge toward the spiritual life. Because the opposition of the human heart against the progressive impulse in evolution originates from the luciferic beings, and because these beings will launch their attacks when, as it were, they already have human beings by the throat, the resistance of human hearts will inevitably be strongest at such times. Hence we shall understand that the very reason why the most important truths for humanity have lived on from earlier times is that the strongest opposition had to be contended with. Anything that differs only slightly from what is customary in the world will rarely encounter fierce opposition; but what comes into the world because humanity has long been thirsting for but has not received it, will evoke violent attacks from the luciferic forces. Therefore a "society" is really nothing more than a rampart against this understandable attitude of the outside world.[1] Some form of association is necessary within the framework of which these things can be presented, with the feeling that in those to whom one speaks or with whom one is in contact there will be a certain measure of understanding, whereas others who have no link with such an association are oblivious of it all.

Everyone believes that what is given out in public is their own concern and that they have to pass judgment upon it; they are instigated, of course, by the luciferic forces. From this we realize that it is indeed necessary to promulgate anthroposophy and that anthroposophy is bringing something essential into our age, something that is longed for by the present thirst and

---

1. It must be remembered that this lecture was given in 1912 and that at the Christmas Meeting of 1923, in Dornach, when Rudolf Steiner became its president, the Anthroposophical Society was given a new foundation and constitution.

hunger for spiritual nourishment and—whatever the circumstances—will come in some form or other; for the spiritual
powers who have dedicated themselves to the goals of evolution see to it that this shall happen.

We can therefore ask: What are the most important truths
that should be implanted in humanity at the present time
through anthroposophy? Those for which there is the most
intense thirst are the most essential. The answer to such a
question is one that can very easily be misunderstood. For this
reason it is necessary, to begin with, to make a distinction in
our minds between anthroposophy as such and the Anthroposophical Society. The mission of anthroposophy is to bring
new truths, new knowledge, to humanity, but a society can
never—least of all in our age—be pledged to any particular
tenets. It would be utterly senseless to ask: "What do you
anthroposophists believe?" It is senseless to imagine that an
"anthroposophist" means a person who belongs to the Anthroposophical Society, for that would be to assume that a whole
society holds a common conviction, a common dogma. And
that cannot be. The moment a whole society, according to its
statutes, were pledged to a common dogma, it would cease to
be a society and begin to be a sect. Here is the boundary where
a society ceases to be one in the true sense of the word. The
moment someone is pledged to hold a belief exacted by a
society, we have to do with pure sectarianism. Therefore a
society dedicated to the principles described in these lectures
can be a society only from the aspect that it is under the right
and natural spiritual impulse. It may be asked: "Who are the
people who come together to hear something about anthroposophy?" To this we may reply: "Those who have an urge to
hear about spiritual things." This urge has nothing dogmatic
about it. For if a person is seeking for something without saying, "I shall find this or that," but is really seeking, this is the

common element which a society that does not wish to become a sect must contain. The question: What does anthroposophy as such bring to humanity? is quite independent of this. Our reply must be: Anthroposophy as such brings to humanity something that is similar to all the great spiritual truths that have been brought to humanity, only its effect upon the human soul is more profound, more significant.

Among the subjects we have been studying in our lectures there are many that might be considered less distinctive from the point of view of something entirely new being presented to modern humanity. Nevertheless they are fundamental truths which do indeed penetrate into humanity as something new. We need not look very far to find this new element. It lies in the two truths that really belong to the most fundamental of all and bring increasing conviction to the human soul: these are the two truths of reincarnation and karma. It may be said that the first thing a really serious anthroposophist discovers along the path is that knowledge of reincarnation and karma is essential. It cannot, for example, be said that in Western culture, certain truths—such as the possibility of becoming conscious of higher worlds—present themselves through anthroposophy as something fundamentally new. Everyone who has some knowledge of the development of Western thought knows of mystics such as Jacob Boehme or Swedenborg, or the whole Jacob Boehme school, and they know too—although there has been much argument to the contrary—that it has always been considered possible for a human being to rise from the ordinary sense-world to higher worlds. This, then, is not the element that is fundamentally new. And the same applies to other matters. Even when we are speaking of what is absolutely fundamental in evolution, for example, the subject of Christ, this is not the salient point as regards the anthroposophical movement as such; the essential point is the form which the subject of Christ assumes when reincarnation and karma are received as truths into human hearts. The light thrown upon the subject of Christ by the truths of reincarnation and karma—that is the essential point.

The West has been profoundly concerned with the subject of Christ. We need only be reminded of people in the days of the gnosis, and of the time when esoteric Christianity was deepened by those who gathered under the sign of the Grail or of the Rose Cross. This, then, is not the fundamental question. It becomes fundamental and of essential significance for Western minds, for knowledge, and for the needs of the religious life only through the truths of reincarnation and karma; so that those whose mental horizons have been widened by the knowledge of these truths necessarily expect new illuminations to be shed on old problems. With regard to the knowledge of reincarnation and karma, however, all that can be said is that tentative indications are to be found in Western literature, for example, at the time of Lessing, who speaks of the subject in his essay, "The Education of the Human Race." There are also other examples of how this question has dawned upon minds of a certain profundity. But for the truths of reincarnation and karma to become an integral part of human consciousness, assimilated by human hearts and souls, as in anthroposophy—this is something that could not really happen until our own time. Therefore it can be said that the relation of contemporary people to anthroposophy is characterized by the fact that certain antecedents have enabled reincarnation and karma to become matters of knowledge to them. That is the essential point. Everything else follows more or less as a matter of course if someone is able to acquire the right insight into truths of reincarnation and karma.

In considering this aspect of the subject, we must also realize what it will mean for Western humanity and for humanity in general when reincarnation and karma become matters of knowledge that take their place in everyday life as other truths have done. In the near future, reincarnation and karma must pass into human consciousness far more deeply than was the case, for example, with the Copernican view of the universe. We need only remind ourselves of how rapidly this theory penetrated into the human mind. Only a comparatively short period in world history has elapsed since the Copernican view of the universe first became generally known, yet it is now taught even in the elementary schools. As far as the effect upon the human soul is concerned, however, there is an essential difference between Copernicanism and the anthroposophical world conception, insofar as the latter is based on the fundamental principles of reincarnation and karma. To be able to characterize the difference, one really needs a group of anthroposophists, of people who come together with good will to understand, for things would have to be said that would cause too great a shock to those outside the anthroposophical movement.

Why is it that the Copernican view of the universe has been accepted so readily? Those who have heard me speak of it or of modern natural science in general know well that I pass no derogatory judgment on the modern scientific mode of thinking. Therefore in characterizing the difference I shall not be misinterpreted when I say that for the acceptance of this world picture, limited as it is to the presentation of external relationships and conditions of space, an epoch of superficiality was necessary! The reason why the Copernican theory took root so rapidly is none other than that for a certain period of time human beings became superficial. Superficiality was essential for the adoption of Copernicanism. Depth of soul—that is to say, the exact opposite—will be necessary for acceptance of the truths of anthroposophy, especially of the fundamental truths of reincarnation and karma. If, therefore, the conviction grows in us today that these truths must become a much stronger and more widespread influence in the life of humanity, we must realize at the same time that we are standing at the boundary between two epochs: one, the epoch of superficiality, and the other, the epoch when the human soul and human heart must be inwardly deepened. This is what must be inscribed in our very souls if we are to be fully conscious of what anthroposophy has to bring to humanity at the present time. And then comes the question: What form will life take under the influence of the knowledge of reincarnation and karma?

Here we must consider what it really means for the human soul and heart to recognize that reincarnation and karma are truths. What does it mean for the whole of human consciousness, for our whole life of feeling and thinking? As anyone who reflects about these things can realize, it means no less than that through knowledge the human self grows beyond certain limits to which knowledge is otherwise exposed. In past times it was sharply emphasized that human beings could know and recognize only what lies between birth and death, that at most they could look up with faith to one who penetrates into a spiritual world as a knower. Such conviction grew with increasing strength. But this is not of very great significance when regarded merely from the aspect of knowledge; the subject becomes really significant when we pass from the aspect of knowledge to the moral aspect. It is then that the whole greatness and significance of the ideas of reincarnation and karma are revealed. A very great deal could be said in confirmation of this but we will confine ourselves to one aspect.

Think of the people belonging to earlier epochs of Western civilization and the great majority of those living at the present time. Although they still cling to the belief that our inner being remains intact when we pass through the gate of death, it is imagined—because no thought is given to reincarnation and karma—that the human being's spiritual life after death is entirely separate from earthly existence. Apart from exceptional phenomena to which credence is given by those with spiritualistic leanings, when the dead are alleged to be working into this world, the current idea is that whatever takes place when someone has passed through the gate of death—be it punishment or reward—is remote from the earth as such, and that the further course of a person's life lies in a quite different sphere, a sphere beyond the earth.

Knowledge of reincarnation and karma changes this idea entirely. What is contained in the soul of someone who has passed through the gate of death has significance not only for a sphere beyond the earth, but the future of the earth itself depends upon what a person's life has been between birth and death. The earth will have the outer configuration that is imparted by the human beings who have lived upon it. The whole future configuration of the planet, as well as the social life of people in the future, depends upon how human beings have lived in their earlier incarnations. That is the moral element in the ideas of reincarnation and karma. A person who has assimilated these ideas knows: According to what I was in life, I shall have an effect upon everything that takes place in the future, upon the whole civilization of the future! Something that up to now has been present in a limited degree only—the feeling of responsibility—is intensified, imbued with the deep moral consequences of these ideas. A person who does not believe in them may say: "When I have passed through the gate of death I shall be punished or rewarded for what I have done here; I shall experience the consequences of this existence in another world; that other world, however, is ruled over by spiritual powers of some kind or other, and they will prevent what I have within me from causing too much harm to the world as a whole." A person who realizes that the ideas of reincarnation and karma are based upon reality will no longer speak like this, knowing that human lives will be shaped according to what they have been in earlier incarnations.

The important point is that the fundamental ideas of the anthroposophical conception of the world will pass over into human souls and hearts and arise as moral impulses undreamed of in the past times. The feeling of responsibility will be intensified to a degree that was formerly impossible, and other moral insights will necessarily follow. As human beings learning to live under the influence of the ideas of reincarnation and karma, we shall come to know that our life cannot be assessed on the basis of what has taken expression in one life between birth and death, but that a period extending over many lives must be taken into account.

When we encounter other people with the attitude that has prevailed hitherto, we feel sympathy or antipathy toward them, strong or moderate affection, and the like. The whole attitude of one person to another in the present age is in reality the outcome of the view that life on the earth is limited to the one period between birth and death. We live as we should after all be bound to live if it were true that human beings are on the earth only once. Our attitude to parents, brothers, sisters, friends, is colored by the belief that we have only one life on the earth.

A vast transformation will take place in life when the ideas of reincarnation and karma are no longer theories held by a few people as is the case today—for they are still largely matters of theory. It can truly be said that there are numbers of people today who believe in reincarnation and karma; but they act as if there were no such realities, as though life were actually confined to the one period between birth and death. Nor can it be otherwise, for habits change less quickly than ideas. Only when we introduce into our lives right and concrete ideas of reincarnation and karma, only then shall we find how life can be fertilized by them.

As human beings we begin life in the circle of our parents, brothers and sisters, and other relatives; in our early years those around us are there owing to natural factors such as blood relationship, proximity, and the like. Then, as we grow up, we see how these circles expand, how we enter into quite different connections with human beings, connections that are no longer dependent on blood relationship. These things must be seen in the light of karma and then they will illumine life in an entirely new way. Karma becomes of significance only when we grasp it as a concrete factor, when we apply to life itself the facts brought to light by spiritual-scientific investigation. These facts can, of course, be discovered only by such investigation, but then they can be applied to life.

An important question in connection with karma is the following: How does it come about that at the beginning of the present life, for example, we are drawn to certain others through blood relationship? Spiritual-scientific investigation of this question discovers that as a rule—for although specific facts come to light there are countless exceptions—the human beings with whom we came to be associated involuntarily at the beginning of our life, were close to us in a former life—in most cases the immediately preceding one—in middle life, in the thirties; then we chose them voluntarily in some way, drawn to them perhaps by our hearts. It would be quite errone-ous to think that the people around us at the beginning of our present life are those with whom we were also together at the beginning of a former life. Not at the beginning, not at the end, but in the middle of one life we were associated, by our own choosing, with those who are now our blood relations. It is frequently the case that a marriage partner whom someone has chosen deliberately will be related in the next life as father or mother, or brother or sister. Spiritual-scientific investigation shows that speculative assumptions are generally incorrect and as a rule contradicted by the actual facts.

When we consider the particular case just mentioned and try to grasp it as a finding of the unbiased investigations of spiritual science, our whole relation to life is widened. In the course of Western civilization things have reached the point where it is hardly possible for people to do otherwise than speak of "chance" when thinking about their connection with those who are blood relations. They speak of chance and in many respects believe in it. How indeed could they believe in anything else if life is thought to be limited to one period only between birth and death? As far as the one life is concerned they will of course admit responsibility for the consequences of what was brought about. But when the Self is lead beyond what happens between birth and death, when this Self is felt to be connected with other people of another incarnation, they feel responsible in the same way as they do for their own deeds in this life.

The general view that people have themselves karmically chosen their parents is not of any special significance, but we gain an idea of this "choosing" that can actually be confirmed by other experiences of life when we realize that those whom we have chosen so unconsciously now, were chosen by us in a former life at an age when we were more conscious than at any other, when we were fully mature.

This idea may be unpalatable to some people today but it is true nevertheless. If people are not satisfied with their kith and kin they will eventually come to know that they themselves laid the basis of this dissatisfaction and that they must therefore provide differently for the next incarnation; and then the ideas of reincarnation and karma will become really fruitful in their lives. The point is that these ideas are not there for the sake of satisfying curiosity or the like, but for the sake of our progress. When we know how family connections are formed, the ideas of reincarnation and karma will widen and enhance our feeling of responsibility.

The forces that bring down an individual human being into a family must obviously be strong. But they cannot be strong in the person now incarnated, for they cannot have much to do with the world into which that individual has actually descended. Is it not comprehensible that the forces working in the deepest depths of the soul must stem from the past life, when the individual brought about the connections by the strong impulse of friendship, of "conscious love," if it may be called so? Conscious forces prevailing in one life work as unconscious forces in the next. What happens more or less unconsciously is explained by this thought. It is most important, of course, that the facts should not be clouded by illusions; moreover the findings of genuine investigation almost invariably upset speculations. The logic of the facts cannot be discovered until afterward and nobody should allow themselves to be guided by speculation, for that will never bring them to the right vantage point. They will always arrive at a point of view that is characteristic of a conversation of which I have already spoken. In a town in South Germany a theologian once said to me: "I have read your books and have realized that they are entirely logical; so the thought has occurred to me that because they are so logical their author may perhaps have arrived at their content through pure logic." So if I had taken pains to write a little less logically I should presumably have gone up in the estimation of that theologian, because he would then have realized that the facts presented were not discovered through pure logic! Anyone, however, who studies the writings thoroughly will perceive that the contents were put into the form of logic afterward but were not discovered through logic. I at any rate could have done no such thing, of that I assure you! Perhaps others might have been capable of it.

Regarded in this way, these things bring home to us the deep significance of the idea that the most important impulses proceeding from anthroposophy must necessarily be moral impulses. Emphasis has been laid today upon the feeling of responsibility. In the same way we might speak of love, of compassion and the like, all of which present different aspects in the light of the ideas of reincarnation and karma. That is why through the years it has been considered of such importance, even in public lectures, always to relate anthroposophy to life, to the most immediate phenomena of life. We have spoken of "The Mission of Anger," of "Conscience," of "Prayer," of the different ages in the life of the human being, approaching all these things in the light in which they must be approached if we assume that the ideas of reincarnation and karma are true.[2] The transforming power of these ideas in life has thus been brought home to us. In reality the main part of our studies has been to consider the effect of these fundamental ideas upon life. Even if it is not always possible in abstract words to convey the significance of reincarnation and karma for the heart, for conscience, for the character, for prayer, in such a way that we are able to say: "If we accept the ideas of reincarnation and karma, it follows that. . ."—nevertheless all our studies are illumined by them. The important thing for the immediate future is that everything—not only the science of the soul but the other sciences too—shall be influenced by these ideas.

––––––––––––––––––––

2. See: *Metamorphoses of the Soul.*

If you study a lecture such as the last public one on "Death in the Human Being, Animal, and Plant," you will see that it was a matter of showing how people will learn to think of death in plant, animal, and the human being when they discern in themselves that which stretches beyond the single human life. It was made clear that the Self is different in each case. In the human being there is an individual Ego, in the animal there is a group soul, and in the plant we have to do with part of the whole planetary soul. In the case of the plant, what we see outwardly as dying and budding is to be conceived of simply as a process of falling asleep and waking. In the animal there is again a difference; here we find a certain degree of resemblance to the human being inasmuch as in a single incarnation a self comes into some kind of evidence. But in humans alone, who themselves bring about their incarnation, we realize that death is the guarantee of immortality and that the word "death" can be used in this sense only in the case of the human being. In using the word "death" in the general sense, therefore, it must be emphasized that dying has a different signification according to whether we are speaking of the human being, or animal, or plant.

When anthroposophists are able to accept the ideas of reincarnation and karma in the form in which we must present them, as distinct from earlier conceptions such as are found, for example, in Buddhism, their studies will lead them quite naturally to other things. That is why our work has been mainly devoted to studying what effect the ideas of reincarnation and karma can have upon the whole of human life. In this connection it is obvious that the work of any anthroposophical association or society must be in conformity with the mission of anthroposophy. It is therefore understandable that when we speak about questions that may seem to those outside anthroposophy to be the most important, the fundamental truths are the basis upon which we speak of matters closely concerning every Western soul. It is quite conceivable that some people might accept from anthroposophy those things that have been described today as fundamentally new and not concern themselves at all with any of the differences between the various religions, for the science of comparative religion is by no means an essential feature of modern spiritual science. A great deal of research is devoted to the subject of comparative religion today and in comparison with it the studies pursued in certain societies connected with spiritual science are by no means the more profound. The point of real importance is that in anthroposophy all these things shall be illumined by the ideas of reincarnation and karma.

In another connection still the feeling of responsibility will be essentially enhanced under the influence of these ideas. If we consider what has been said today about blood relationship and companions once freely chosen by ourselves, a certain antithesis comes into evidence: What in one life is the most inward and intimate impulse, is in the next life the most outwardly manifest. When in one incarnation our deepest feelings of affection go out to certain human beings, we are preparing an outer relationship for another incarnation—a blood relationship, maybe.

The same principle applies in another sphere. The way in which we think about some matter that may seem to us devoid of reality in one incarnation will be the most determinative factor in the impulses of the next; the quality of our thinking, whether we approach a truth lightly or try to verify it by every means at our command, whether we have a sense for truth or a tendency to fanaticism—all this, as the result of assimilating the ideas of reincarnation and karma, will have a bearing upon our evolution. What is hidden within our being in the present incarnation will be most in evidence in the next. A person who tells many untruths or is inclined to take things superficially will be a thoughtless character in the next or a later incarnation; for what we think, how we think, what attitude we have to truth—in other words, what we are inwardly in this incarnation, will be the standard of our conduct in the next. If, for example, in this incarnation, we too hastily form a derogatory judgment of someone who if really put to the test might prove to be a good or even a moderately good person, and we carry this thought through life, we shall become unbearable, quarrelsome people in the next incarnation. Here is another illustration of the importance of widening and intensifying the moral element in the soul.

It is very important that special attention should be paid to these things and that we should realize the significance of taking into our very soul what is really new, together with everything else that with the ideas of reincarnation and karma penetrates as a revitalizing impulse into the spiritual development of the present age.

My aim has been to bring home to you the importance of reflecting upon what constitutes the fundamentally new element in anthroposophy. This of course does not mean that an anthroposophical society is one that believes in reincarnation and karma. It means that just as an age was once ready to receive the Copernican theory of the universe, so is our own age ready for the ideas of reincarnation and karma to be brought into the general consciousness of humanity. And what is destined to happen in the course of evolution will happen, no matter what powers rise up against it. When reincarnation and karma are truly understood, everything else follows of itself in the light of these truths.

It is certainly useful to have considered the fundamental distinction between those who are interested in anthroposophy and those who oppose it. The distinction does not really lie in the acceptance of a higher world, but in the way thoughts and conceptions change in the light of the ideas of reincarnation and karma. And so today we have been studying something that may be regarded as the essential kernel of anthroposophical thought.

FURTHER READING

by Rudolf Steiner

At the Gates of Spiritual Science. Hudson, NY: Anthroposophic Press, 1986.

The Being of Man and His Future Evolution. London: Rudolf Steiner Press, 1981.

Between Death and Rebirth. London: Rudolf Steiner Press, 1975 (o.p.).

The Evolution of Consciousness. Sussex, England: Rudolf Steiner Press, 1991.

Facing Karma. Hudson, NY: Anthroposophic Press, 1975.

Karmic Relationships: Esoteric Studies, 8 vols. London: Rudolf Steiner Press, 1955-72.

Life between Death and Rebirth. Hudson, NY: Anthroposophic Press, 1968.

Manifestations of Karma. London: Rudolf Steiner Press, 1976.

Man's Being, His Destiny, and World Evolution. Hudson, NY: Anthroposophic Press, 1984.

An Outline of Occult Science. Hudson, NY: Anthroposophic Press, 1972.

Stages of Higher Knowledge. Hudson, NY: Anthroposophic Press, 1967.

Theosophy. Hudson, NY: Anthroposophic Press, 1971.

Theosophy of the Rosicrucian. London: Rudolf Steiner Press, 1966.